# THE TRUSTED ONE

*An insider's view into the secret
world of guardianship*

ANNIE B. WAGNER

**BALBOA.**PRESS
A DIVISION OF HAY HOUSE

Balboa Press books may be ordered through booksellers or by contacting:

Balboa Press
A Division of Hay House
1663 Liberty Drive
Bloomington, IN 47403
www.balboapress.com
1 (877) 407-4847

Print information available on the last page.

ISBN: 978-1-9822-3916-9 (sc)
ISBN: 978-1-9822-3918-3 (hc)
ISBN: 978-1-9822-3917-6 (e)

Library of Congress Control Number: 2019919578

Balboa Press rev. date: 12/10/2019

This is for you, Sophie, Isabella, Stephan, and Violet
And for you, Maddy

# AUTHOR'S NOTE

This book, while based on true events, is not meant to betray medical or professional confidences, or to single out any individual or group of individuals for criticism. There are many similar circumstances affecting crisis for vulnerable adults, not only in the south, but all over the United States. It is meant to portray my own experiences. I use mostly the feminine, but "her" story is just as often "his" story.

I have taken the liberty of changing all names and places to protect the privacy and rights of people. I know my clients want me to tell this story to help others.

By telling our story, my clients and I are making a plea for change in the guardianship system. This system must better support both vulnerable people in America and the many dedicated guardians trying to protect them, recover them, and enhance their lives. Americans need to rely on this public service; it needs to be more trustworthy for all of us.

# CONTENTS

# INTRODUCTION

# How Can We Know Who to Trust?

**December 2017**

I met three women on a train. I was seated with them in the dining car. The Amtrak train was traveling overnight from the chilly north to the warm south. We talked into the night, telling stories of why we were there. Each woman at the table was traveling toward or away from a crisis for an elder. My calling!

I explained that I was an elder advocate and I was returning from a two-year struggle to keep my best friend, Stephan, with Parkinson's and dementia as happy as possible. Stephan had asked me to keep him as free as possible, even though he now needed twenty-four/seven care. I loved him. I understood him, so I achieved his wish for as long as I could. It was expensive in every way and worth it.

Now I was traveling from way up north. Two days ago, I closed on the sale of Stephan's highly mortgaged house. I felt much relief and much satisfaction at having succeeded on what he wished for: Freedom and financial stability.

These three fellow travelers told me their stories of crisis and deeply pushed me to finish writing about my experiences as a guardian because they, each in a different way, needed to find their way to people and services they could truly trust.

Each woman needed help. Not that they were helpless people. They were amazing women! Ella was a retired Disney executive and her friend Julie was a lawyer turned writer on a spiritual path. Julie and Ella were coming back from a court appearance in Washington DC. Ella's brother was dying in hospital when his hired nurse married him bedside so she could inherit his fortune. Ella protested. Then the hired nurse turned around and accused Ella of being the bad guy and of interfering in her brother's wishes. So, the spiritual-path writer, Julie put on her lawyer cap to support her friend to ride the train to Washington DC to testify as defendant at her brother's so-called wife's court case against her.

Ella was forced to defend herself in an exploitative scenario. "How could my brother's friends let this happen to him on his death bed? How come I'm the bad guy!"

These two women found great lawyers, rounded up witnesses and even though they lost the money to his nurse, they succeeded in saving the family homestead for family.

The stress of being accused was uncomfortable for Ella. She was forced to defend against a bully who used that old tactic: "The best defense is a good offense." Julie saw Ella's need for help and so supported her friend during a long ordeal. It did not enhance the friendship. Ella suffered from arthritis. She needed a cane and lived in pain. Ella was grumpy. She entered a cocoon and stopped talking with Julie the day she exited the train. Their homes in different towns, Julie tried to stay in touch, but ultimately the exhausted silence between those two friends prevailed.

My friendship with Julie, the lawyer turned writer on a spiritual path, continues today. She has been curious, encouraging and wise during this writing process. She has requested ideas and strategies from me when her elderly neighbors and loved ones have needed support. I have recommended trustworthy colleagues in her area and I have presented to Julie some of my elder advocacy dilemmas too. She is brilliant, humble and collaborative.

The other dinner companion was Stephanie, a wedding planner. She told us she was traveling to a town just south of mine. She was traveling toward her estranged father who was an alcoholic. He had moved in with his parents, her grandparents. They died and now her father was unable to cope in their home. As well they left tons of money and Stephanie was worried. Should the money be in a trust? Did he need a guardian? As well, she was worried about how to connect with him or even… did she want to connect with him? I gave her the name of a lawyer I know for sure has integrity, who does not overcharge, who will be able to collaborate with her and her father to find solutions. She was walking into a possible guardianship for her father so I explained that she had choices. I gave her the name of a very wise geriatric care manager/guardian I trusted who I knew would try to avoid guardianship. This care manager would rather mediate and develop a plan without incurring expensive court costs and public records in establishing a guardianship. I gave her "who to trust".

This dinner and sharing into the night offered solace and inspiration. I felt soothing resonance and any loneliness I felt from standing strong in advocacy for Stephan and for others before him seemed to heal. These women validated me and loved what I was doing. We were healing one another. It was one of those times when I knew I was exactly where I was meant to be.

I shared more stories of keeping my best friend out of an institution going on two years. I told them more about my experiences over years of being a guardian. I saw good guardians everywhere who mentored me with generosity and compassion. I also witnessed cruelty and lack of respect for elders that made me burn and made me want to speak out.

I was guardian to a woman living with schizophrenia. She needed a guardian, and that collaboration was successful. However, I have a desire to remove the word "guardian" from elder care in the way that elders in crisis do not need to lose their civil rights. Europe does not do it this way. Germany would not dare to remove anyone's civil rights because of full awareness of the crimes and discriminations committed against people with disabilities during the Nazi period of 1933–45. Why are we in America doing it?

Many elders in crisis have recovered and stabilized under guardianship. However, our system can take away their civil rights making it too tempting for a guardian to assert authority over someone and minimize a person's right to self-determination. An advocate must care to invest the substantial hours required to properly know and collaborate with their clients. Elders are often too weak to fight when placed against their wishes inside nursing homes or dementia units with locked doors. Our system makes it too convenient to imprison elders inside "safe" locked facilities, due to time constraints by a guardian or the need for a paying customer.

Guardians are forced to run an independent business and they are often sleep deprived from heading off a crisis at any time of day or night. Guardians must accept indigent wards that cannot pay them and so guardians hope to find a few paying clients that will allow them to stay afloat financially. At the same time guardians must avoid any whiff of conflict of interest in managing the money of their wards. Guardians can be sued by disgruntled family members or others because guardians, like parents, are legally responsible for their vulnerable adults. Guardians can be chastised by the court because an auditor for the court found a few dollars missing from the accounting. Guardians hold insurance and bonds to protect themselves. They do the overly "safe" thing to cover their own ass in the tricky legal/medical/adult protective services system. Guardians are forced to go for so-called safety first. Guardianship is supposed to be a last resort solution. Many elders headed for difficulty or crisis don't benefit from this guardianship system.

Elders can find themselves unsafe in our world today. They are not sure who to trust. Friends and relatives can lock an elder up because they can't give them the time of day and some may wish to hasten their death and therefore gain control of their assets. I have seen an elder get angry about this and try to fight. Then she was labeled difficult, a pain in the ass, paranoid, and locked up with hastily diagnosed dementia. This is a cycle of events that needs to be more visible. And it needs to be stopped.

## Earlier in 2017

I gave a talk at an independent retirement community coffee hour. I talked about my goals to keep my friend, their fellow resident, Stephan living with dementia, free as long as I could and how creative it had to be and how time consuming and expensive it was, and how important it was for Stephan and for me inside our vow of trust.

As I was leaving one elderly gentleman whispered to me, "It is secretly our worst fear to be sent to a locked ward."

We both knew his fear was based in truth.

It is crazy to lock up our elders. It is only for *our* convenience. It is indecent.

## Credentials

Today I work in a small assisted living facility. I practice emotional care for twenty people living with various kinds of dementia. I was trained in this special awareness in authentic 'being with' those living with dementia by Dr David Sheard and his fellows at Dementia Care Matters in the UK. I speak of the training in detail in Chapter Nine. Some of the residents I work with now are very active and others are dying. All are living, feeling beings, holding hands with me and often holding hands with each other. This is an evolvement for me that stems from my own guardianship style. I consider guardianship a sacred calling. There are many empathetic advocates and a few bad apples in a system based in fear. This story shows the need for change and, ultimately, ideas for change in a broken guardianship system.

I am sixty-five years old. I do not have any wards of the court at this time by choice. I hold my bonds and certifications to remain connected to the governing bodies and associations that oversee the integrity of guardianship. I hope this memoir can contribute to a process that can decipher how to create a more trustworthy guardianship system with much more humanistic practices. I have clients and family members who have asked me to "mentor" them. I love that word as it suggests supported decision making, collaboration and enhancing lives. I attend to my loved ones and clients who need my support in order to avoid a crisis. They have needed the temporary support of an advocate because they are having surgery, or they are trying to remain home with worsening dementia, or they can no longer avoid entering the residential long-term care system.

I have more wisdom and experience advocating for vulnerable people than I had twenty years ago when I started advocating for family members. Many people become professional guardians because they have cared and advocated for their loved ones, and they carry that love into the calling.

I now have ten years of experience as a professional advocate. My first few years as a guardian were a learning curve revealing to me, my talents and my deficits. I have had to learn how to confront carefully the nasty things people do because I do not seem to be able to develop much of a protective shield. My face refuses to lie. I live as honest a life as I can since I know my feelings show on that face. I like this quality in me. There is a confidence at my core. I have the talent to perceive deeply what I see. My vulnerable ones feel it. Hence, they will let me hold their hand and they will, most importantly, collaborate with me. I have always known that "power" was a sacred responsibility to others. People's feelings are involved. Authority over the life of a colleague or the life of a vulnerable soul in trouble is a responsibility. I feel sick when people use and abuse their power. Most guardians will resist abusing the power the court does give.

I have felt responsible to the "goodness" of the calling. I know some of my colleagues have breached the ethics standards, ruining it for "trust".

These are stories of my personal experience inside real, much-needed and warranted guardianships, and my experience witnessing unwanted guardianships and unwanted control over elders. These stories advocate for vulnerable people, especially elders. These stories also advocate for guardians, who are not well supported in the system. I hope to answer some worries about "How can we know who to trust?"

# CHAPTER ONE

# How I Became A Guardian

I had a long career behind the scenes in film development. I was briefly an actress. However, being shy, I preferred working behind the scenes with writers on screenplays and casting films in order to procure financing. I achieved a satisfying career. I retired in 1999. My hobby then was renovating houses. I have continued to create beautiful houses.

## Uncle Leo

In the year 2000, Uncle Leo had a stroke and two weeks later, Leo was starting to become aggressive with Aunt Thelma. Thelma called the police and then she called me.

It was urgent. The police took Leo to the hospital strapped to a gurney and then put a guard on him. The hospital case managers were pressuring Thelma to hurry up and place Leo in a locked ward. I helped Thelma with Leo's crisis for the next six months. I tried to find the best situation for Leo to recover his brilliant mind back from his stroke. His body was not handicapped by his stroke; however, he was losing his memory.

I got on the phone, advocating, persuading people to take Leo on, challenging for the best care over and over. I visited Leo to check on him, to hold his hand, to observe his level of wellbeing, to mentally stimulate and challenge him. I moved Leo around because I was disappointed when care didn't match the promises, when care was mostly less-than. People in the dementia business seemed strangely neutral. They made excuses for neglecting to provide care for him. "He was sleeping." or "He was in the bathroom". They were not caring for Leo and they were placating me; this was frustrating.

I was running into one crisis after another with Leo's situation. He was known to the system with the label 'Violent'. He was trapped in locked wards. Staff approached him with fear. I was not afraid of him and he never hurt me. However, my attempts at advocacy in his defense met with dead ends.

Recently, Leo had escaped his facility. I spontaneously clapped "Hurrah!" The nurses were furious with my reaction. I was fed up with his staff. I was rebellious too, in-your-face proving to the directors of the almighty Dementia Innovation Center how clever Leo was to escape. I wanted to fight for his brilliance. "See he is brilliant to escape." They were lying about the progressive care they promised him. They never intended to help Leo progress after his stroke, as they'd advertised. The Dementia Innovation Center was only a fancy, expensive piece of architecture.

They decided it was dementia and there was no attempt at improvement to be found for Leo. It was only a warehouse, after all. I hired outside people to work with Leo. One man played the piano in the lobby with Leo beside him. Then they played with a remote- controlled toy race car. Leo started telling everyone this was his son. We had known that a person living after a stroke can improve, and today we know a person living with dementia is still highly intelligent. My instinct was, dementia or stroke, I must try for meaning in Leo's life. Even when money was no problem, I could not find what he needed. A woman on the ward was called Thelma like Leo's beloved wife, our Thelma. Leo followed her around all day every day. This was discouraged, but it was not harming anyone. It was not even harming our real Thelma because she understood, Leo's dedication to her doppelganger.

I celebrated the day Leo broke out, but he was stuck in the system, labeled a troublemaker and violent by fearful staff. He was being restrained by antipsychotic drugs because he hated the shower. No one wanted to sooth *Leo's* fear of falling water. Today we know how to help him accept a shower. He had to be locked up, only because we had not yet learned how to help him *live* with dementia.

Leo wanted to take his rifle and walk in his beloved fields and forest one last time and then shoot himself. The problem was he was violent with Thelma *before* he had a chance to do it. As time passed in the torture of his abyss, I dared to think, too bad he did not go out and shoot himself. Thelma and I both knew Leo wanted to commit suicide. It was (and is) against the law to help him achieve it.

Leo was begging Thelma to go free. After a year in captivity with no gains in cognition, brilliant Leo was deeply unhappy, and it became useless to subject Thelma to the two-hour drive to the disappointing Dementia Innovation Center. We moved Leo to a nursing home closer to Thelma. A month after that,

Thelma and I let the nurses give him Haldol, which we had fought for so long, hoping he would improve.

After he was doped up, restrained by Haldol (a nursing home's best friend), Leo lasted three weeks and died of pneumonia from the inaction caused by the drug. This is not unusual. I saw it a few years later with my friend, Carol, who had end stage breast cancer in another nursing home.

No matter how hard we tried, we failed to improve things for Leo. This is how my path to becoming a guardian started. I needed things to improve.

I have studied and learned how so-called behavioral problems in someone living with dementia can be solved. Each person in this situation of aging or dementia wishes for freedom and collaboration. Now, I have a chance to do it right.

The system has been deadly slow in changing to new, more humanistic ways, which are considered radical. How are love and true understanding and finding meaning in life radical? Care staff are taught to hide behind tasks, to stay objective and to give neutral care. Controlling behavior in staff is condoned as normal, and even subtle controlling behavior toward vulnerable people hurts their feelings. Can it be considered emotional abuse? My teacher, Dr David Sheard, of Dementia Care Matters believes it is.

Well-meaning people who work in dementia, simply lack education about their effect on vulnerable souls. They are not trained to this awareness: the ways in which they create loneliness in their residents.

After Leo died, I became POA for more of my family and friends. I saw that I was good at being with my loved ones when they needed me. My brothers and sisters relied upon me to step in on any emergency for our parents. My stepfather had dementia, and I helped my mum coordinate his care at home. And I studied.

Who am I now in early retirement? I took some aptitude tests to better understand what I might be good at now. I visited with my friend Peter of Heartriver.org. He intuited my spirit: "A deep resonance with contributing to the survival of humanity." Gee-whiz! I only wanted a meaningful retirement job. And yes, Peter. Thank you. I do feel the big picture.

Community organizers were looking to test people for scholarships. They trained people to stand up and fight for underserved communities. I have a strong need for justice in the world. However, the overriding quality that came out of my aptitude test was not only "justice"; it was stronger toward "mercy."

Then I was introduced to the 16 Personalities test. The test pointed to me the "Advocate (INFJ-T)" which indicated that the right path might be as an elder advocate:

"People with this personality type tend to see helping others as their purpose in life. Advocates can often be found engaging in rescue efforts and doing charity work. However, their real passion is to get to the heart of the issue so that people need not be rescued at all." NERIS Analytics Limited: https://www.16personalities.com/infj-personality

It felt right. I then went to a conference where geriatric care managers learned the latest innovations in medical and elder care matters. There were many speakers with a wealth of knowledge about the latest trials for a dementia cure, special ways to protect an elder's money in various trust accounts, and new ideas about multi-generational living experiments. I felt I was in the right place. I was inspired.

This professional choice felt like a calling. I wanted to study geriatric care management. I talked to care managers; I started asking questions about how I could become one.

A care manager, Anita suggested that one way into geriatric care management certification was by first becoming a court-appointed guardian. I studied books about geriatric care management, and I went to guardianship classes at the local college.

## Guardianship School

There were many required fiduciary skills and certifications for this calling. To become a professional guardian in the southern USA, the first credential was to complete a forty-hour course on guardianship and pass an exam at a community college. This course was taught by a practicing guardianship lawyer. He persuaded the court "auditor" to visit our class. His job was to frighten us and hold us accountable. He required book keeping skills that accounted for every penny passing through the "guardianship of the property." This was about maintaining exactly the ward's assets, conducting the bill pay and other functions of daily living required by a guardian.

I was finger printed, investigated, my credit checked. All people coming in contact with the ill or the disabled must be cleared. I was required to have a $50,000 Blanket Bond. I was given the license to practice guardianship and this paperwork was placed in files with the clerk of the court in the counties where I was to have wards.

Six months later, I became a National Certified Guardian (NCG) which means that I have undergone a much more complex training and taken a much more advanced exam. I have sworn to stringent ethics and standards which guide me well, as the job is all about making the best possible decisions with and for a vulnerable adult.

But really it takes time to become a good guardian. Wisdom will develop through experience. A guardian enters a person's most sacred rights and freedoms.

## First day of guardianship school:

"Recover them!" said Dylan C.

He was a lawyer and my guardianship teacher.

He continued, "The most important job for a guardian is to recover their wards.

Recover their rights.

Recover as much quality of life as possible.

The job is to get them out of crisis and get them out of guardianship."

This I understood, and it ignited me.

Their freedom: work for it.

I loved it!

# CHAPTER TWO

❖❖❖❖❖

# The Guardianship of Sophie T.

A few months after I passed my exam, Mary S. gave me my first ward. Mary was a very experienced, no-nonsense guardian, administrative in style, who I met at the monthly guardian association networking breakfasts.

Sophie T. was living with schizophrenia. She had been complaining about Mary to the guardianship lawyer. After ten years of being first Sophie's power of attorney and then having to turn that into being Sophie's guardian, Mary admitted she was tired. Because neither Sophie nor Mary were enchanted with the other, I received my first guardianship. I was called the successor guardian. Mary asked me if I could put some attention to enhancing Sophie's life and that was exactly up my alley.

Mary told me that Sophie and her father had moved south from up north to be warmer and closer to relatives. He promptly died, leaving Sophie orphaned. Unable to live in a real world without support, Sophie felt she should have died with him.

On July 24, Sophie was "Baker Acted" because she was unruly and suicidal. This meant that she was placed on a secure mental ward for seventy-two hours.

I first approached her in the emergency room as she was being processed, and she smiled at me. "Ann? You're my new guardian! You're pretty."

Sophie was tall, thin, and sixty-three years old. She had been diagnosed with schizophrenia when she was nineteen, at a hospital near the prestigious University of New England that Sophie had attended for two years before her first extreme episode. After that first hospitalization, her schooling stopped, and Sophie had lived with her father until he died ten years earlier.

Now, Sophie was talkative and ladylike. Her face was long, her chin pronounced, and she had quite a few wrinkles. Was it the years of anti-psychotic medications that caused her face to appear odd? I could see her vast intelligence and her interest in the world. Her eyes glistened. She was smiling and pleased to meet me. Were they sure she was suicidal? Or was it that, at this moment, she felt safer in a hospital than in the world at large?

Sophie was hungry, so I went to the lobby café and bought her a chicken Cuban sandwich. Even though she explained that she was allergic to every food item and medication known to mankind, she ate the whole thing! She waved and smiled as they pushed her gurney toward the locked ward.

I made another visit with Sophie inside the psych ward during her seventy-two-hour plus-a-few-more-days stay. She complained that she couldn't smoke there. She was charming and chatty. She was not the least bit disturbed by her environment. It was my first time in a locked psych ward, and

I was trying hard, probably not very successfully, to control my nervous fear.

On July 30, through the guardianship lawyer, the court granted my "letters of guardianship" just in time for me to pick up Sophie at the hospital. I took her back to her assisted living facility for the mentally ill. It was official. I was Sophie's guardian.

I remembered my brother and sister-in-law the day they had their first baby. Their faces were ashen; they were overwhelmed at the idea of caring for the tiny, helpless infant in their arms. I didn't have any children. Now I felt the same shock at the responsibility of care. A ward is a responsibility, a big one. But a ward is not a love child. A ward can be dangerous, troubled, and demanding of attention. A ward could be difficult. I love a challenge ... don't I?

It took me two weeks to study Sophie's files and finances, and then write the required plan for her. I visited with her several times to get to know her better and see what was needed. Sure, I got to see where she was "out to lunch", and I also liked her a lot.

After that, I wrote the initial plan for the "person". The court needs to approve of what I intend to provide for my ward in the area of medical care, socialization and living arrangements. I studied the financials and wrote the initial plan for the "property": the ward's assets and income and the budget: how the ward's money will be spent. I passed these two reports to the paralegal for the guardianship lawyer, who must agree with my assessments before presenting it to the court.

## The ruthless scrutineer

I was naive, judgmental, fervently advocating for the ward to be treated well. I was an overly diligent beginner, and the idealism was never to disappear.

GUARDIAN OF THE PROPERTY: fiduciary of Sophie's money.

I had run my own non-profit art gallery, so I understood enough about accountability. I had responsibility for large sums of money by working as a producer in the film biz, but I had few learned skills as a bookkeeper and so I had to work at it. No one knew much about me in this new town, in this new state. As a beginner in a new realm, I wanted to become known slowly by good work in the present.

I had a plan for my first ward. I was going to enhance her life and, at her request, help her find a life outside her mental health community.

I received, as required, the financial paperwork on Sophie from Mary, the guardian, and Noah K., the lawyer.

THE LAW: Mary will be obligated to hold copies of this information for three years.

I looked at the numbers and thought to myself, "How could a lawyer and a guardian spend $25,000 in a year leaving the ward now almost indigent?"

I suspected them of paying themselves too much money.

What world did I come from? Do people not have to make a living doing this? I studied hard. Where did her money go?

Sophie had a few stocks. Mary had sold Sophie's condo and placed her in an assisted living facility.

THE NUMBERS:

Penny's House, the ward's assisted living facility for the mentally ill, was $1,300 a month, $15,600 a year.

Her medications were covered by Medicare Extra Help, a plan available to the one hundred percent disabled.

Sophie's cigarettes and personal needs: $100 a month, $1,200 a year. Renovation costs, as the condo was full of mold and mildew: $5,000. Lawyers for the closing of the sale of the condo and creating the guardianship fees over the year: $5,000 (half the price of the usual).

There it was: $25,000 in one year.

Nobody had stolen anything or acted in the least unethically. Tons of work, disgusting work too, went into securing Sophie from harm. She would run in the streets in the middle of the night, frightened that a man whispering at her from behind the wall was trying to get into her apartment. She had been living in squalor all by herself.

After a year under guardianship, Sophie now had $10,000 left in the lawyer's trust. I asked the lawyer to leave the $10,000 for our ward because she needed it. I don't think the lawyer liked me for this. I don't think Mary, who was to become my mentor guardian, liked this either, because she smelled my idealism and perhaps my refusal to understand how rare it was to be paid as a guardian. She was insulted because she was giving me a gift and I didn't know it. "Take the money!" was written all over Mary's face.

But I was a brand-new guardian who was obligated to take pro bono cases. I couldn't take a dime knowing Sophie would run out of money in less than a year.

I requested that Sophie become a pro bono guardianship. This lawyer didn't speak to me. (He didn't speak to guardians on pro bono cases?) It was lonely. I spoke only to the paralegal. My letters and questions to the lawyer got no response.

I was to stretch that ten thousand dollars to over two years. And then the lawyer rewarded my work by asking me into his office. I understood. I had to earn his trust.

The assisted living owner, Colin, gave me a deal a few months later and we were able to pay just $700 a month for assisted living (most of Sophie's social security check). Mary, my mentor guardian, was impressed that I got Colin down from $1,300 a month. It was not that hard. I asked. Colin said yes. Then, with permission of the court, I sold some stocks; it was enough to buy a cremation. I spoke with our sixty-three-year-old Sophie about her wishes at her death. She said she would like to be cremated.

THE LAW: No one can be cremated until either they themselves or their children give permission. Otherwise they must be buried. The guardian, through the guardianship lawyer, must ask the court to approve a prepaid cremation. It is pleasing to agencies such as Medicaid that an almost indigent ward has a prepaid funeral. One less expense for the state to worry about.

If a ward is able to communicate, one must collaborate and ask them for their wishes and try to give them what they want, as long as it doesn't harm them or others, or jeopardize their safety. Freedom versus safety is always in the balancing act in guardianship.

Sophie definitely needed a guardian—no argument from her there. She was collaborative, and I gave her hours of attention. Psychotherapy was to prove useless because Sophie acted up in front of the therapist, who she felt was an authority figure. She exhibited fear every time.

Sophie requested a computer class. I arranged it and took her to her first class. She was afraid of people because she'd been sheltered with her father and inside mental facilities most of her life. She gave me a lot of dirty looks for the first fifteen minutes.

The gentleman who taught the computer class took her under his wing. He later donated a computer to her, and I got Sophie an email address.

I started placing attention on Sophie's medical difficulties and quality of life. I began by taking her to horseback riding therapy as she had been an expert rider as a young girl. This was a commitment all right, as it took an hour to drive out to the farm. I believe the attention I gave Sophie by driving her to the farm started to erase her profound loneliness. She loved the horses, but it reminded her of how far downhill she'd come since the time when she was a champion jumper and the head of her 4-H club. In her youth, she was in charge of something in life. Mary had told me she felt, because Sophie was so brilliant, she was very much aware of her long fall into mental illness. It was devastating to Sophie.

I took Sophie to Dr. F., a psychiatrist affiliated with Charlotte, my favorite MSW (master's degree in social work). I wanted to know if there were new drugs we could try; I didn't want to give up on the idea of a better life for Sophie. I had heard that a new drug, which required work in the form of blood tests to monitor the safety of the drug, had caused surprising normalcy in some people living with schizophrenia.

Sophie acted up terribly in the session with Dr. F. The psychiatrist made faces. (Hadn't she seen a schizophrenic freak out before?) The doctor shot me a look that said, "Why did you bring this insane person here?"

Dr. F. changed the meds; she hoped Sophie would feel better on Depakote. That was an old tried-and-true medicine for maintaining function in the world. I wanted a more ambitious response. I wanted to try for a chance at remission.

"What about the newer medications?" I asked.

"They're too new," Dr. F. said. "Sometimes dangerous for an older person."

I pushed for a private room for Sophie. I pushed again and

then again. Finally, Colin agreed that Sophie could move to a private room in a woman's house separated from the main building but still behind a fence on the property, which was in a slummy part of Saint Sandton. Inside the building were state of the art electronic systems and clean renovated décor, but Colin didn't want the outside to look great. He wanted it to look like a slum: scrubby grass, no flower gardens, salmon-colored stucco like a lot of low rent homes on the street. Colin was positive no one would steal from a house that looked like theirs, especially with scruffy-looking, scary-looking people milling around in the parking lot. People with mental illness do have a certain look that frightens people who aren't used to it.

I bought a cell phone for Sophie for her safety. The area and some of her fellow residents were a little worrisome. I felt she was at risk without a phone. I didn't wish to restrict her walking in the area on her way to the library downtown, which was only four blocks away. Her personal freedom which included walking free was a calculated risk.

After a few months, Sophie began to appear listless. Her birthday was upon us and Christmas would arrive a few days later. Sophie was very low, despondent. I got her a digital camera.

She opened the gift and set the camera down, disappointed, "I wanted a Timex watch."

A few days later, I got a call from Penny's House. "Sophie's in crisis. Then another call: "We think Depakote is making her despondent."

Colin wanted to Baker Act Sophie. I phoned Dr. F. with a request to stop Depakote. I called Colin to say I didn't want Sophie in Memorial Hospital. But if she had to go to a hospital, I wanted it to be Manor Mental Hospital. I fought Colin on the idea of committing Sophie.

"Are you sure?" I asked. "It's almost Christmas."

"Exactly," Colin said. "Christmas is hard. We work diligently here to make a celebration, but it's not like many families turn up." Colin made a decision. "Let's wait a few days."

The next day was the Christmas party. I brought Sophie Jojoba oil for her skin. I took her new cell phone for repair and got it working again. I could see that Sophie was depressed. She usually took pride in her clothes. Now she was dirty and poorly dressed.

Many phone calls occurred over Christmas time. "Sophie's not well. She can't settle down. She won't take her meds. She won't eat or drink. She's angry."

"Christmas hurts my feelings," Sophie said, telling me what Colin already knew so well about his gang.

Now Colin would not delay. He wanted to Baker Act Sophie as fast as possible. If I didn't come, the staff would call an ambulance.

I picked up Sophie in my car. Colin instructed me not to disclose to Sophie where we were going. I told her after we got to the hospital. Sophie didn't protest when we arrived at Manor Mental Hospital. She knew the routine. She was Baker Acted per Colin's instructions. She allowed me to hold her hand. A few hours later, I left her locked up there. At least, a good perk for her, they had a fenced exterior yard where patients could smoke. This was the main reason I wanted her at this particular hospital but I was to learn that they were willing to try harder for Sophie's possible remission as I wanted.

The next day, I picked up some of Sophie's clothing. I also gathered her long medical history for the doctor. I wrote him a long letter seeking new treatment for her. I met with a nurse and delivered clothing, cigarettes, and my letter explaining what I hoped for. I got permission to see Sophie on the ward, and as I entered the lock-up, I heard the nurse saying, "I knew Sophie had a good one." I knew I was a good guardian for Sophie too.

She looked extra sleepy. I handed her a chocolate bar, and she showed me around. Sophie stayed there, not for the regulatory seventy-two hours, but for two full weeks.

That would be the last time Sophie would be Baker Acted. Manor Hospital agreed to try a promising new drug as both Sophie and I had requested. They also referred her to a behavioral health clinic right around the corner from her assisted living facility. We could walk over for a session of talk therapy or a side effect complaint at a moment's notice. This was like a touch stone. Sophie tortured herself and she felt safer now.

Setting things up was time consuming administratively. I had to get Sophie's new prescription worked out. The prescription for Zyprexa was for two months, not one month, and the pharmacy refused to deliver the medication without another prescription, clearly stating "two months". Well okay. Guardians run around crossing t's and dotting i's all the time.

After adjusting to the new medicine, Sophie was her busy, curious self once more. Sophie had sleep apnea, so I arranged a sleep study. She spent the night at Memorial Hospital's sleep unit. They called at 6:30 a.m.

"She's ready." I told them it would take me thirty minutes to get there. "Well, we'll have to keep her here, then."

The night before, when I brought her in at 7:30 p.m., they were pretty frightened of her. They asked if she was an elopement risk. They put her at the end of the hall so the other patients wouldn't be disturbed in case she acted up. I told them she wasn't dangerous to others, just tortured within herself.

I arrived at 7:00 a.m.

"Can you tell me how it went?" I asked. The nurse didn't know any details.

"She has sleep apnea," she said, "and refuses to wear the mask. They put it on her while she was sleepy. Maybe they frightened her. Dr. Adelle will call you."

I drove Sophie and a C-PAP machine back to the assisted living facility. Sophie told me she didn't have money.

I went out to find breakfast and collect myself. I sat in the car, wrote two checks, one to have Sophie's phone reconnected because she'd used that money for cigarettes instead, and one for her allowance.

After a few weeks, Sophie abandoned her C-PAP machine. At least we tried.

I was very impressed with Colin, the man who owned the assisted living facility. He advocated for all mentally ill souls, all over the southern USA. Colin was a strong, sensitive, and courageous person.

One day he asked me, "Are you a fighter or a lover?"

"I care. A fighter, maybe. I'm a lover for sure. I would love to know how to fight better." I didn't yet know what I was in this new world. I loved Colin for his big advocacy.

He asked me if I had a bachelor's degree and said he wanted to offer me a job there. That was a big vote of confidence, but I didn't have the degree, and I didn't say more about my amazing career in the past. I didn't really want a job there, but I very much admired the facility.

Sophie went on to study philosophy, music, and opera at elder classes all over town. Now, two and a half years later, Sophie was volunteering at the library bookstore, and at the senior's center. A special friendship program provided volunteer friends to people with mental illness. Blessing! Sophie and her volunteer friend, Emily went to the theater together and they went for coffee together.

Eventually Sophie spoke with me more deeply about her feeling that she didn't deserve to live. Being useful at the library, being an usher at the theater, and having a parent-like friend in Emily had changed her feelings from acute to tolerable. Guardians can achieve this. The court asks us to develop trust, enhance lives and recover people. Sophie smiles often. I'm proud of how Sophie and I have collaborated.

After two years, Sophie didn't have any money beyond her social security. So, I applied for a free Medicaid cell phone for her safety. She didn't have much for her personal needs. Her uncle and cousin lived far away. They sent her something at Christmas, so I asked them to consider helping with her monthly allowance. They have.

By including her uncle in the collaboration, by writing, sending pictures of Sophie in horse therapy, and learning that he cared, I was able to request support for her. Before that, Sophie didn't have anyone.

Many wards have absolutely no one. Our Sophie has relatives in this very town of Saint Sandton where she lives, but they want nothing to do with her. Sophie looks funny. She has difficulty navigating authority figures. She can act up. But she is very intelligent, generous of spirit, and a very fine conversationalist. Medications for schizophrenia improve every day. I keep up with research, hoping for a cure.

I support my clients and wards to do as much as they can and to make the decisions that they can make, as long as they are not dangerous decisions for themselves or for others.

Oh dear, but "dangerous" is a relative term and the balancing of risk and freedom are always on the mind of a guardian. "Do I keep brilliant Sophie from volunteering at the library because she has to walk four blocks in a slummy part of town? Some guardians would say absolutely no to volunteering. I say yes and make sure her cell phone is working which is not guaranteed because she would rather buy cigarettes than pay the variety store the twenty dollars for continuing cell service. No, I am not disappointed. She makes me smile. I 'get' her. I know her schedule so I can check on her: did she safely arrive at her assisted living facility for the mentally ill after her happy volunteer job? Yes, because other knowing volunteers, seeing her paranoia and vulnerability and not so safe neighborhood, walked her home. Beautiful!

*"In spite of everything, I still believe that people are really good at heart." Anne Frank from The Diary of a Young Girl*

# CHAPTER THREE

## The Kidnapping of Dorothy G.

After a month in my new guardianship business, I had networked enough in health care meetings and luncheons to make some friends. Charlotte, my favorite Master's of Social Work (MSW), asked me to look into guardianship for a few of her clients. She was already helping me get the most support I could for Sophie. Charlotte had taught me how to navigate Medicaid on behalf of my clients; the application process can be daunting.

Karen D., an assisted living facility administrator, asked me if I would consider taking her resident, Isabella C., as my second ward. Dalton, Isabella's brother, was a pharmacist. He knew Charlotte, Westbrook being a small town, medically affiliated colleagues relied upon one another.

Both Charlotte and Karen complained about the cookie cutter approach of the well- established guardians, June and Marianne and David. Guardians in Westbrook seemed territorial. At an educational conference, I moved close to say hello to June, Marianne, and David. They eyed me, consciously moved away, turned their backs.

Wow, I sensed I wasn't going to get any collaboration

in Westbrook. I was sure I'd only get the wards that these established guardians refused to take on. I accepted this as par for the course. Once I'd proven myself on difficult and pro bono cases, the lawyers and the court would then look favorably upon me, and only then would I receive a case that could actually pay me. I accepted this too. I was building a service based in trust. It had to go slow and sure.

In Saint Sandton, to the south, guardians were cautious but much more generous in spirit. Guardians helped each other and there seemed to be an honor system. They shared paying clients and pro bono clients, gently keeping one another afloat in each of their own entrepreneurial businesses. I felt supported. As did the two other new guardians, my classmates.

I had two guardianship school buddies in Saint Sandton. Melanie and Roy started guardianship businesses at the same time as I did. We bonded. I had fantasies of having a business together because we had complimentary qualities. Roy had a Master's Degree in Administration. Melanie had been a paralegal, a lawyer's assistant. And me? I listened intently and I naturally wanted to hold someone's hands. I wanted our wards to heal and recover as much self-determination as possible.

Melanie was a cancer survivor and wanted a professional job that was less structured. All three of us found out this job was very hard with very long hours. Correction: not enough hours in the day. Melanie, Roy, and I didn't realize how grueling a guardianship business could be.

In Saint Sandton, there was no feeling of the competition for a rich ward that I sensed in Westbrook. In Westbrook, I saw a guardian, Corine, get kicked off a case. Why? Because the case was a multi-millionaire and belonged to the most established guardian in Westbrook—David. Okay? Not Friendly. I didn't hope for any future in Westbrook, even though I lived there. I had my trusty Prius, and the half-hour drive to Saint Sandton was not costly.

There was only one guardian in Saint Sandton who didn't talk to me. Philip looked at me as if to say, "I can't believe you will ever make a good guardian." He was laughing at me. Did I look like a lightweight? Philip had not yet felt my steel core, my sense of home within myself, my creative ability to solve problems. He actually looked me up and threw it in my face? "Actress?" I had not mentioned my past to anyone.

We were at a health care networking luncheon, when I agreed to talk with a local parish nurse about her client. Philip knew there was no money in it and thought I was a fool to listen so intently to a nurse, who was troubled about a mother/daughter duo in a trailer park down the road. Philip laughed at me.

I felt his slight. While my look back at him didn't say, "I'll show you," it did say, "Reserve judgment. I'm not sure who I am in this either, but let's wait and see."

Philip had a BMW. Did he have only wealthy wards? Was that right practice? Maybe he had an inheritance? Philip became Roy's mentor guardian and they were a good match. Roy had a master's degree from Princeton, and who was I anyway? Philip showed Roy what not to do, pointing at me because I'd agreed to take the parish nurse's charity case. I was not willing to tell

Philip or anyone who I'd been in my past lives, but I trusted my experience was equal to a master's degree.

A stranger came up to me that same day. Bob introduced himself as an insurance salesman.

"My mother is a guardian." He said.

He continued, "I don't know why anyone would want to be a guardian. Last week they called my mother to the hospital at 2 am. Last week two of her wards died and a third tried to kill himself with the cord from his oxygen tube. Really I can't figure why anyone would want to be a guardian."

Yikes! Okay. Were those cases hopeless? Perhaps I misspelled my calling. If we take away two letters in guardian, "sounds like" you will find me. I am a garden? And in the garden, we can solve a crisis and we can find our way back to dignity, to belonging somewhere, to recovery, and back to self-determination. That is what I hoped for. Was I dreaming?

I took the case of Dorothy and her daughter, Tina, and collaborated with Abby, the parish nurse. Abby's heart was deeply committed to humanity. She was warm and I immediately embraced her as a friend. We recognized one another; we confided in one another. I was grateful for a real friend. I would deeply need her friendship and her belief in me a few years later.

Abby's church pastor also became my counselor when I felt troubled by my cases. His church was way cool. The pastor conducted well attended services for several families from elders to the elders' great grandchildren. The altar often became a stage for the pastor's rock band. I attended those rock band rejoicing hymn services with my two clients, who were both in Abby's bible study class.

## Dorothy G.

Dorothy, age eighty-eight owned a trailer. Tina, Dorothy's daughter, age forty-five, and her two dogs were living in this single-wide trailer with her mother. The trailer stood on a rented lot costing $453 a month. The prior month Tina had neglected to pay the lot rent when she decided to have her car fixed instead. Her mother's social security check was $950. Tina received $200 from unemployment insurance. Tina appeared to have a separate account that her mother didn't know about. Church gossip informed Abby the parish nurse that, in the past, Tina had taken expensive vacations in Europe using her mother's savings, which were all gone now, and that Tina drank to excess all day after she dropped her mum at elder daycare.

For five years, Abby had been helping and caring for Dorothy, her fellow parishioner and part of her bible study class.

Tina had been Baker Acted the previous month for depression and spent three days in a locked mental ward. With Tina out of the trailer, this gave Abby a chance to see how terrible the living conditions were for Dorothy. Tina's two dogs lived there too. If Dorothy opened the door to the trailer, the dogs would escape. With a slow gait and a walker for balance,

Dorothy would not be able to catch the dogs, so all three were trapped inside. Abby was very worried about Dorothy.

We went to work for Dorothy. Abby and I retained a cool young lawyer in Saint Sandton. Mary, my mentor guardian, helped us too. She gasped when I told her Dorothy was in trouble. She had known Dorothy before she retired, as the pharmacy assistant in the drugstore who knew everyone by name. We all worked to see if we could get Dorothy into the Medicaid program for the assisted living facility that had accepted her a year before.

We succeeded in re-enrolling Dorothy at The Oaks of Saint Sandton. Her daughter, Tina, was furious, when we told her that her mother had been accepted to live at the Oaks. I sat down with Tina to see if I could help her. I tried to persuade her to reassure her mother that she, Tina, would be all right if Dorothy left to live at the Oaks. Tina was not able to give her mum the reassurance Dorothy needed.

A week later, a room was offered to Dorothy. She signed a power of attorney, naming me. I promptly used it to cancel the debit card Tina was using because that money needed protecting to pay Dorothy's room and board. I brought Dorothy from her elder daycare after lunch to sign in at the Oaks.

After Dorothy checked in, Abby and I wanted to take her to the trailer to visit Tina and pack her clothes. Dorothy was tired, so the pastor stayed with her. Abby and I went to talk with Tina and pack Dorothy's clothing. Dorothy asked us to pick up her telephone and several items from home; she made a list.

Dorothy was shaky. She had wanted to wait a few more months, when Tina might get a roommate. We knew she'd been delaying for a whole year. We did some fundraising at the church to pay the lot rent for a few months so Dorothy could relax about her daughter's safety.

When Abby and I went back to the trailer park to pack some of Dorothy's things, Tina refused let us in. She refused to give us anything, including Dorothy's health cards, identification, clothing, and any of the items on Dorothy's list. Tina insisted Abby had kidnapped Dorothy and called the police. Tina was a fragile soul in a ferocious personality.

I explained to the police that Dorothy was in her right mind and had voluntarily signed herself into the Oaks. The policeman nodded as if he knew Tina and Dorothy; he asked me and Abby to leave.

The next day, Tina came to take her mother back home. The Medicaid planner, the pastor, me and the administrator gathered quickly in the board room with Tina and Dorothy and we reasoned with them. Dorothy sided with her daughter, saying she was coerced. I knew Dorothy was afraid of her daughter. Tina was invited to stay for lunch with her mother. Dorothy decided to keep her room. I had to report every detail of the events because, if we went to court, I had to show what happened. If Dorothy persisted in agreeing with her daughter accusing us of kidnapping her, saying that she was coerced into signing papers against her will, we would go to court.

I continued to attempt to help Tina. My administratively talented fellow guardian, Roy, had agreed to help Tina with the application process for social security disability insurance for mental illness for her depression. I wanted to introduce him and tell Tina that her rent was paid. Tina refused to speak with me or Roy.

Tina refused to visit the Oaks or support her mother's transition.

She held her mother's identification and medical cards for months. She called her mother and raged at her a few times a week. Dorothy felt pressured to return to the trailer because Tina wanted it, not for Dorothy's well-being. Tina wanted her mother's social security check. THE LAW: government annuities, like social security checks must benefit the recipient and no one else.

It became too uncomfortable to keep the power of attorney and I resigned from it at the bank. However, I succeeded in stopping Tina from using her mother's debit card, therefore her social security check, for her own personal needs, and that stuck.

Dorothy remained at the Oaks and I continued to help and comfort her for a year without having power of attorney or being her guardian, or anything at all. I contributed extra kindness. Abby and I operated with no help from Tina.

As we proceeded, I bought Dorothy a second-hand reclining chair. And had it sanitized. Who knew that furniture could be placed in a special chamber for twenty-four hours to kill any bugs? The church supplied décor for her room, pictures, cute curtains and cushions. Dorothy's fellow parishioners donated clothing of all sorts and I took Dorothy shopping for new undergarments. We became friends and she confided in me, at last, that she was glad to be at the Oaks. There was love and moral support flowing from the Oaks as well. They agreed to help Dorothy without her identification cards. They helped me replace them eventually.

The Oaks was one of the finest continuing care community in Saint Sandton. It used to be the charity home for the poor, but it was so good with care for the elderly that families with money place their loved ones there too. They formed a powerful board of directors for this non-profit and raised a lot of money, so poor elders still had a very fine place to live when they needed assisted living, a nursing home, or memory care. Wealthy elders were not charged the steep prices of the national assisted living mega-companies, and all-around fairness and humanity continued for all residents. No one could tell who had money and who did not. That was a good thing. The Oaks became my favorite elder community, and I was grateful working with Dorothy on the inside so I could learn more deeply about the Oaks.

Finally, because Abby and I failed to foster a connection with Tina, after a year and at my request, Mary became Dorothy's power of attorney. She was able to get inside the trailer and retrieve Dorothy's clothing and mementos. Mary, my very experienced mentor guardian, was known in the community. She had a big rolodex. She found a grooming place that donated its services for cleaning up the two puppies. They were as dirty as the trailer in which they lived with Tina. Those dogs were never taken outside to go to the bathroom, so the smell and disintegration inside the trailer led us to feel very sorry for all, especially fierce and fragile Tina. We couldn't imagine how Tina and the dogs were still alive. Mary sent a hazmat cleaning company to recover the trailer.

Abby, "the kidnapper," wrote a letter of prayer, persuading Tina to come visit her mother once more. Tina was finally rescued by a taxi driver she met when he was in down south on vacation. He took her to New York, and the trailer was sold.

A Note: In each chapter, I describe my whole experience with one ward or client. Over time. I do this for clarity and so each client can fully tell their story. The fact is all my clients and wards came to me within a few months and so I worked with them simultaneously. For me five cases were all consuming and I took measures to keep myself whole. It was work, paperwork, banking work, meeting the needs of each crisis work. I loved it, but I can understand how a guardian with thirty cases or more, could either burn out or do a less than adequate job. Guardians come in many different styles. I was dedicated and so I spent more time with each person under my wing, than most. I became busy and exhausted caring simultaneously for the ones I write about in the following chapters. After two years I had worked with five wards or clients and I could not take on more.

# What I learned from my mentor guardian, Mary

"What does it mean to *hold space* for someone else? It means that we are willing to walk alongside another person in whatever journey they're on without judging them, making them feel inadequate, trying to fix them, or trying to impact the outcome. When we hold space for other people, we open our hearts, offer unconditional support, and let go of judgement and control." *By Heather Plett*

When we can "hold space" for someone, we can hear them better. Our elders and vulnerable adults feel this kind of listening reassuring. It becomes easier to find the necessary trust with a guardian and to share their true fears and wishes.

Abby and I consulted with my mentor guardian, Mary because we wanted to be sure Dorothy *wanted* to go to assisted living, before we started the process rolling. Mary met with Dorothy. I sat with Mary when she "held space" for Dorothy. Mary was ever so gentle. Dorothy responded with her answer because it felt safe: Even though Dorothy was worried about her daughter she longed to be in the stability of assisted living.

**Finding trust:** Mary, a good guardian will "hold space" for a person in crisis.

# CHAPTER FOUR

# The Guardianship of Isabella C.

Karen D. phoned me up to ask me to see an Isabella C. I had spent time touring Karen's facility and I saw how Karen, a great administrator, made all the difference in care for residents. She knew every detail about her fifty residents and made decisions about their safety and medications and life enhancements all day every day. Her office was always open, and her little dog was the invitation. Hey, I came to use that open door too, when I faced problems and needed a second opinion on the care of my vulnerable ones.

The building was old, but it was right on the river and the views were wonderful.

"Isabella could use a tender approach," Karen said.

I could do a tender approach! Karen had me. Her flattery caught me like a fish! Being an expert at perceiving people, she saw that I was either a real sucker, so new I didn't know what I was facing, or potentially, a good guardian for Isabella C.

Translation: no other guardian would touch Isabella with a ten-foot pole, because she was too angry. I wanted to know why she was angry. I was curious by nature. I wanted to give.

Isa's brother, Dalton, was her guardian and desperate to get out of it. I did see it would be a challenge, but I thought, "Well, I'm new. What other kind of cases am I going to get? The ones nobody else wants. Okay. I'll play, and with gratitude." Dalton had been her guardian for eight months. He was unhappy, and I was looking to see if it was in Isa's best interests for me to become her legal guardian.

Karen and I found Isabella on the back porch, smoking and watching the river. Karen introduced me at 4:15 p.m. on Friday the 13th and I spent fifty minutes with Isa.

Isa told me her brother had agreed to let her have two packs of cigarettes a day, so Isa was chain smoking. It was striking to me that she was so young. She was only forty-two years old. Most of her fellow residents were elderly. I wondered if a more age-appropriate residence with care existed. Could I collaborate with Isa for her wellbeing?

I had not seen much information on Isa. I knew she was in pain. There was a long list of drugs. She was in a wheelchair. She looked dirty and disheveled, with long tangled hair. I saw underneath her finishing school refinement showed. I saw her distress.

Isa had petitioned the court for restoration of capacity. She was unhappy with "imprisonment". Her court hearing had been the previous day. She'd informed the judge she felt she'd made only one mistake: she accidentally overdosed.

Isa told me guardianship was a racket. A money-making scam. She had watched her money flow out to lawyers and yet had been stopped by her brother from buying face cream. Her cream was Olay Regenerist. Would I score her cream back from her evil guardian? Would I help her stop all this nonsense with her civil rights and the confiscating of her freedom? I stayed silent.

"I want to go to Europe," she said. She was looking for an escape route.

I knew Isa was not permitted to leave this court circuit, this county, let alone run away to Europe. Isa was furious at guardianship. I did not agree that it was a money-making scam, but I was surprised at how expensive the guardianship process seemed.

Isa did not agree with the past judgment of incapacity. She did not disagree when I told her she seemed vulnerable. So, we had agreement on "vulnerable."

After she said she hated shrinks of all sorts, I suggested she might benefit from neuro-linguistic programming therapy, which is also called accelerated learning (through the subconscious). She was intrigued.

The next morning, I visited again. Isa showed me the letter she wrote to the judge.

I learned that her friend, Jan, was willing to take the guardianship, but after court on Thursday, the judge didn't agree to it. I learned that the lawyer and her brother had fought over money. So, the most established guardianship lawyer in Westbrook had been fired due to the exorbitant fees he charged.

("That lawyer is off the case!" Isa gloated.) I was aware that on Thursday a lawyer, Owen T., had come onto the case. He was fair-minded, Dalton had told his sister, and reasonable, financially speaking.

Isa disliked Dr. Marma and Dr. Derko, the court-appointed evaluators of her capacity. They had declared her to lack capacity. She felt they presented a conflict of interest with her brother, who worked beside them. Her brother was a pharmacist in Westbrook.

"My brother hates me. He must have influenced them!" (I was recording the information Isa was throwing out at me so I could verify it.)

Isa's mother was at another assisted living facility. Isa didn't want to be near her mother because she felt that she was totally self-centered. Isa liked swimming in a pool. The ocean and salt water were too much of a hassle. She said her niece, Wendy, got $50 a month to care for the dog. Isa wanted better food for her Chihuahua, Bruiser, and wouldn't bring her dog to the assisted living facility because "he's a happy dog and this is a morgue." Bruiser was a tiny dog. She wanted the judge to know that.

Isa assumed I had contact with the judge. I didn't let her know I was on the periphery.

I was in the shadows and silent, behind any lawyer who was in charge of the case and in charge of me. I had not yet met lawyer, Owen T.

I asked Isa what she was going to be doing with her time?

"Like what do you mean?" she asked, sounding defensive.

"Like volunteer. For example, help animals?"

She perked up. "I would love to volunteer tutoring kids."

She told me her stuff was in storage. She'd stopped teaching primary school three years ago. I attended a bit of her lunch hour with Doris and Hope, the two elders with whom she sat in the dining room. She ordered yogurt for lunch and had a cup of coffee with five sugars. When the food for the others arrived, she showed her disapproval. "See. Too greasy. I rest my case."

Isa continued to educate me about her needs. She wanted to walk again. ("Great!" I thought.) She didn't need physical therapy all the time, only someone to watch so she didn't fall. Only out-patient insurance was left to cover physical therapy. Since her overdose, eight months before, a great deal of physical therapy had been needed.

"Is there a reason I can't have my guitar in my room?" Isa asked.

She believed her brother has been able to cheat both her and her mother out of money because his wife has the same name as her mother. I later learned from Dalton this absolutely wasn't true. He didn't take a dime for being Isa's guardian. I saw that Isa was seriously attracted to the energy of anger and rage. Venting anger was the catharsis for "injustice" done to her. It consumed her. It might even be giving her strength, a semblance of power in her powerless state. However, it was toxic to all those around her.

I felt that Isa was no collaborator. Perhaps with some tenderness that could change. She was only forty-two years old. She had been a teacher at a public elementary school for over ten years. She had been Baker Acted three times in the last three years. She'd had a car accident. She had a subdural hematoma, left untreated for a few months. She had back pain and had endured serious spinal surgery. She had brain damage from lack of oxygen during a suicide attempt, eight months earlier.

Isa kept asking, "How much do you cost?"

"Guardians charge zero to eighty dollars an hour." I explained that I was a manager of affairs, so I always created a budget and my people would pay only what they could afford. I told Isa I was not familiar with her case or finances. I told her, I had seen that the process of guardianship in the courts was expensive, but thankfully the court was equipped to protect her. A guardian would be sworn to protect her and her property from neglect, abuse, and exploitation. That went over like a lead balloon.

A few days later, I dropped in to the legal office of the former lawyer to see why he "resigned" from the guardianship of Isabella C. I told him I was considering taking on the case. He said Isa was capable of calling the newspaper, and the bad publicity a lawyer or guardian might encounter would not be advisable. He said he had advised everyone he worked with not to take the case. I thought this over. He had managed to press a button in me. I didn't want to be in the public eye. I also valued a pristine reputation.

I phoned up Dalton, Isa's brother.

"Dalton," I said, "I can offer you care management for Isa. I would like to work with her. I suggest you stay guardian. I will take the pressure off you, and we can save the lawyer's fees."

The next day he phoned to say, "No thanks."

In the next week, Isa smoked almost two cartons of cigarettes in five days. There was no money in her account at the assisted living facility, and Isa was livid. She was now threatening elders to get out of her way, or she would run them down. She almost succeeded! Karen officially kicked Isa out of the care home. Dalton called me. He accepted my offer to care manage and he would remain as guardian. He offered me $20 an hour. I accepted.

I started working to get Isa a therapist. I also looked to see how many other residents under age sixty there were in assisted living facilities in Westbrook or Saint Sandford. Penny's House, where Sophie lived, had diverse ages, but it was for the mentally ill, not appropriate for forty-year-old ill or disabled adults. I'd found eight people under sixty, and those of us in health care networking were thinking about getting these souls together for a luncheon, and then maybe sort them out, trade around so they might live together. They could then receive group therapy and activities tailored to them. This crisis with Isa had sparked my idea of creating an assisted living facility accommodating a younger clientele in our community. Elders needed protecting from Isa; maybe elders needed to be separate from other young people with chronic illness too.

Part of Isa's rage was justified. But it wouldn't get her anywhere near the freedom she longed for. Her diagnosis should be verified. Why was she in a wheelchair?

Two months after I started helping Dalton with Isa, we went to court with her. Dalton was her guardian. Owen T. was the lawyer for the guardianship. And Larry T. was the lawyer appointed to act for Isa alone. All wards received their own lawyer in a proceeding regarding guardianship or a petition to restore rights.

The judge, having read her letter, addressed Isa's request for restoration of her rights. Isa's friend, Jan had ghostwritten this letter for her. Because of the vast amounts of pain and anxiety medicine she required, Isa didn't have the sharp brain needed to write a convincing argument for the restoration of her rights. After a few questions to Isa, the judge clearly understood that Isa did not write her own letter. But she looked clean and well dressed and had beautiful tangle-free hair. That was my contribution. The judge was not fooled by that either. He wanted to wait and see her again in three months. He was doing the delay strategy, and we all knew it. But I also wanted time to see if Isa could improve or, at least, feel happier.

Two days later, Isa was accused of defecating in the elevator. Karen evicted her, and Baker Acted her to Westbrook Memorial Hospital. Isa was a danger to the elders in Karen's care. This gave me a chance to see the psych ward there. Isa was treated well, and the other patients were more her age.

Karen offered to help me find the right Assisted Living Facility for Isabella. Karen quickly became my favorite assisted living facility administrator because of how she helped me as a sounding board make my decisions regarding Isa. I saw that Karen helped everyone in her large care home. Karen knew Isa was unhappy living with old people. She told me about Care of Westbrook, a psychiatric assisted living facility in Westbrook, which would be more age appropriate for Isa. I drove by and asked around. I walked around inside and absolutely no one was in that care home. It felt like a ghost town. The facility had a seedy reputation. I let Karen know it seemed wrong for Isa. I also consulted with Colin, the owner of Sophie's assisted living facility for the mentally ill. Colin visited Isa at the hospital and evaluated her. He accepted her, and promised to install wheelchair apparatus in her private bathroom.

Seventy-two hours later, the hospital released Isa, and I moved her to Penny's House, Colin's assisted living facility. She hid, facing the corner in the dining room, her back to everyone. She hid for twenty-four hours. A sadder person, I had never seen.

The next day, I took Isa to Dr. F., her new shrink and the head of Isa's mental health ward at the hospital. This was the same psychiatrist who had made faces at Sophie for acting up, but she was also the shrink most recommended by my social worker friend, Charlotte. As well, Dr. F. had just worked with Isa during her Baker Acted stay in the hospital. I hoped Dr F. would persuade Isabella to give Penny's House a chance.

"It's in the worst slum of the city. I'm not safe! It's dirty. It's full of crazy people all staring at me. I can't stand it.

I moved Isa to Prestwick assisted living facility. Dalton felt it was too expensive and Dalton thought Penny's House served her right. Oh dear. I got his anger, but Penny's House was not going to work. Now I hoped Isa would identify with Prestwick's prestigious atmosphere. She was once a finishing schoolgirl and a dressage princess with very ladylike leanings. She was snobby. I hoped this move would support her to become ladylike once more.

## Wings of desire

No one knew what we guardians did, because we were forbidden by law to talk about it. We were a bunch of nobodies with a noble cause, like the angels in *Wings of Desire*, watching over humanity. Our lives were lived in the shadows. The shadows were filled with people washed up in waves of hunger, greed, shame, and fear, abandoned by normal life and so passed into our care. Abandoned people. I jumped to the challenge. Heal them!

"Hey, fairy guardian. Wave your wand. You might succeed ... with one or two," said Mary. She had my number, this wise old mentor guardian. I wanted love to replace all that fear. But then, it was not a word that guardians used: 'love.'

All rooms were papered with fear in these homes and our offices. I saw it and yet I was not convinced that this was a fear-based job. I hoped for hope. But yes, there was a lot of fear.

Love and fear. A fine filmmaker once told me he could simplify life to these two words.

"Love and belonging are essential for life."

– Brene Brown, *Daring Greatly*

I had to make provision for love and belonging for my clients and wards.

Forty-two-year-old Isa lied, manipulated, and ordered people around. She wanted her moment back. We took it from her, after all. Her overdose was interrupted. In a moment of quiet, under her breath, she said it. "Why couldn't they let me go?"

It takes time, focus, and I believe, love to hear such a whisper. Now I knew her goal in life. Her every angry lie was "Give me back my independence. Give me back my life."

Under my breath or maybe only in my mind, I said, "So you can off yourself."

I understood why she was now under guardianship. Her brother was the very battered guardian. He was blamed for everything. He was suspected of stealing and Isa hated him for no reason at all. Dalton had lived through crisis after crisis with his sister and finally he had to do it. She lost her civil rights.

I consider it grave for any citizen of the United States to lose their civil rights. All guardians and lawyers can point out people who would be too dangerous to themselves or others if they had the right to make choices. Unfortunately, Isa qualified.

Isa was such a pain in the ass to people that they couldn't work with her and hoped they would soon forget her; such was the nature of her anger and her hatred of the world. She was a perfect picture of abandonment, self-abandonment, and everyone was going to pay for doing this to her. For keeping her alive!

I got that. Isa wanted the right to kill herself and we couldn't allow it. She would be angry at me too because I knew she was truly a candidate for guardianship. Dalton was still begging me to become her guardian.

It was maddening and exhausting to work with Isa. And I loved her.

On Sunday, I cooked dinner for my friend, the retired judge, and we talked. I was torn about whether to become Isa's guardian. Isa was already so much trouble. She called me ten times a day as it was. If Isa felt that I had power over her, might she not turn against me?

"It might exhaust you to have full responsibility for Isa," my friend said. I did see the risk to my own wellbeing. I hoped Isa would see me as the collaborator and the trusted one I had been for her to date. I hoped Isa would have an epiphany. I hoped I could find the key to her, when she might again find meaning and feel like being alive.

# Accounting my hours for care management for Isabella C.

| | | | |
|---|---|---|---|
| **Mon.** | | Meeting with Owen T., Larry T., Dalton, and me about becoming Isa's official guardian. The gentlemen say please. They complement me and my work. I say a cautious yes. | 1.5 hour |
| **Wed.** | 8:30 a.m. | Pick up toiletries at Walmart. | 0.3 hour |
| | 9:15–11:30 a.m. | Pick up Isa. Go to Larry T. Larry was her own lawyer and wanted to develop trust. | 2.2 hours |
| **Fri.** | 11:30 a.m.– 1:30 p.m. | Bring Isa to the vet for medicine for Bruiser. We visit Bruiser. We visit with Isa's friend, Jan, and invite her to attend court. | 2.0 hours |
| **Mon.** | 7:30–11:00 a.m. | Court day! I help Isa dress and take her to court. | 3.0 hours |
| | | **Total** | **9.0 hours** |
| | | **9.0 hours x $20** | **$180** |

That day, I became the court-appointed guardian for Isabella C. My goal was to try hard to entice Isa back to a life with some kind of meaning. No one knew her real medical history. Why was she in a wheelchair? Now I was allowed to see every document medical, financial and legal.

Isa had been abandoned medically. Many doctors and her brother were exhausted by her. So, I started to form a new medical team around her. I found the right neurologist. Dr. Caitlin asked me to find Isa's medical history, and she searched her profession for other neurologists who might have known our Isa.

Detective work was exciting. I presented my letters of guardianship to the hospital records department, and a few days later I received a very big bundle with many years of medical records.

I unraveled the story from the records. Ten years earlier, Isa was diagnosed with multiple sclerosis. She didn't like that diagnosis, so she changed doctors. Every time she didn't like what a doctor had to say to her, she switched again. She was a loner who drank beer and took many drugs for the pain caused by major back surgery.

"Botched back surgery," Isa told me one day. "I sued the young chick that caused it. She rear-ended me at sixty miles an hour."

Now I was authorized to read her confidential files. Now, I could compare her words with her medical file. Was Isa the one driving in reverse at sixty? Isa got the financial settlement for that. Her pain was real. But maybe her painful back was caused by MS. I wondered to myself if the back surgery was a result of her denial. She couldn't face MS, so she decided she needed spinal surgery. I don't think the back surgeon knew about her diagnosis two years before when he opened her up. No one I knew had any idea about a diagnosis of MS.

The X-rays were scary. Isa's back looked like a ladder of hardware with big, ugly screws sticking out randomly. It was done by a reputable surgeon. But still, she had suspected MS then. Can it be confirmed? Isa could not face her illness. My heart went out to her. How could I get Isa to accept the probability, the certainty? It took me a few weeks to feel out a strategy. I consulted the neurologist, Dr. Caitlin alone, without Isa. The doctor suggested she would start again with Isa. Tests were more advanced now. She could show Isa her brain scan. Because Isa had avoided treatment for ten years, she would need aggressive infusion therapy. It was effective in producing long-lasting remission. Let's try it. There's hope!

I waited at the social security office and, when my number was called, I registered as Isa's guardian, becoming the representative payee for her social security disability check. I dropped in to see Bruiser's veterinarian. Wendy, Isa's niece needed medicine for Bruiser. I gave my letters of guardianship to the vet's office so they would talk with me. I spent an hour at the bank. I opened a bank account named "The Guardianship of Isabella C."

I took Isa to her existing primary care doctor; Dr. A.'s general health evaluation was needed in my initial report to the court. Isa asked the doctor for more sleep meds. She didn't need more sleep meds! She was overmedicated to the max. I questioned her in front of the doctor about her opiates. She became sarcastic and bitchy about my involvement in her life. I dangled a carrot, probably, an ineffective one.

"When you can come off those opiates, you will better be able to live independently."

She changed the subject. Her dog wasn't getting enough attention. She insisted he took Lamictal. Dr. A. explained that Lamictal was a mood lifter for Isa.

"No," she argued, "it's a dog med for inflammation."

Next Isa complained about not having control of her schedule.

"When is your dentist appointment?" Dr. A. demanded, unfairly challenging her with an attitude of his own. Isa couldn't answer (because I managed her schedule). He would ask the neurologist, Dr. Caitlin, to check Isa's memory.

When I dropped her off at her assisted living facility, after fighting me all afternoon, Isa wanted to take me for dinner at C'est La Vie, a Michelin three-star restaurant.

"That's sweet," I said. "No, thank you. You've been there in the past. We can go explore new places another day." I took my leave.

Dr. W., the dentist, performed an examination and consulted with Isa. Isa wanted cosmetic work done on her front teeth.

"Isa is not able to chew," Dr. W. told me, "because she has no back teeth at all." The minimum cost was $4,000. I knew it was Isa's ability to chew or my guardian fees. I choose her teeth, of course.

She was not able to chew! That's why she only ate sweets, yogurt, and whipped cream, and none of the proper food offered by the assisted living facility. Dr. W. did a quadrant cleaning and pulled two rotten teeth. Isa was given antibiotics, special mouthwash, and a toothbrush. I paid $1,500. I drove Isa back to Prestwick and stayed to make sure the nurses were aware of Isa's care needs for dental work.

I started on Isa's initial report to the court. Her change of address needed reporting because I'd changed her care home from Westbrook county to Saint Sandton. I took Isa to Charlotte, master of social work, for talk therapy. I was achieving a bigger team around Isa. I brought Bruiser the dog to live at Prestwick with Isa. She was thrilled.

The medical records revealed much more. Ten years ago:

> Demyelination found. Probable multiple sclerosis. Isa refused treatment by prescription injections.

A few years later, a driving evaluation was done by Dr. Marg B.:

> Isabella walks without assistive devices, adequate vision, decreased reasoning, and judgment with limited insight into her deficits. Decreased recall of previously discussed information. Slow scanning. Cautious driver. She was denied as not safe to herself or others when driving. Further cognitive therapy was recommended.

That same year, Isa's father died. She was very close to her father and was still devastated. A few months after that, Isabella's "disability and behaviors at school" resulted in paid administrative leave. And then a year later, "retirement."

Her overdose occurred two years later. It was now a year after she'd stopped breathing for several minutes. She was probably frightened about her memory.

Now, she was seriously overmedicated.

After a few days, I visited to check on Isa's room and pay her monthly fees. Bruiser was not breathing well. I asked Isa if Bruiser had received his meds. She said no. Isa insisted he was fine. I brought Bruiser to the garden on her lap. We all needed some fresh air.

I chatted with Barbara, the executive director of Prestwick and said I was concerned that the dog, Bruiser, was not well. Isa blamed cleaning staff for products causing Bruiser to struggle for air. I took his meds to the med-tech cart and asked the nurse's assistant if she could administer a dog's meds along with Isa's meds. She smiled. "Yes, I can." Blessing!

The next day, I watched Isa's physical therapy session. Her gait was very odd. I was committed to finding improvements for her. Even though the staff was paid to walk Bruiser, I took him out as I was worried. What a cutie. He seemed a bit better.

The next morning, I got a call from Barbara, the executive director. Bruiser had died! Isa was storming around the lobby, howling, blaming Prestwick and me for his death. He was in her room and she wouldn't let anyone near him.

Poor Isa. I canceled physical therapy. I canceled the dentist. I called Isa's doctors.

Dr. A. did not approve of any extra medication for Isa, but Dr. F. upped her Seroquel.

I was on the phone the whole day. Dalton helped. We sent in Isa's best friend, Jan, to take Bruiser from Isa's room. I negotiated with the pet cemetery. $950!

Jan called me to offer her back yard to bury Bruiser. (Thank you.) She also reported that Isa held Bruiser and kissed him for about an hour. Then Jan was able to take Bruiser out of the apartment. She delivered Bruiser's body to Dr. B. later that afternoon.

Isa was officially blaming me, and Prestwick assisted living facility for her dog's death. She wanted to sue us all. Dalton and I collected data on the dog's diagnosis and found out Isa was told by a vet a year ago that Bruiser had cancer. Isa denied knowing it.

I stayed clear of Isa. I cleaned house and tidied for a birthday party for my neighbor. Isa was leaving hate messages on my phone. I aged ten years. I was very sad about Bruiser dying.

I made empanadas. It was good to see my friends. The next day, I stayed in bed all day. It was a beautiful day. I was trying to gather strength and grace to face the week ahead with Isa. I wasn't looking forward to it. My neighbor fashioned a casket for Bruiser. She varnished a beautiful box from the craft store and lined it with Satin. I bought a lovely stone marker and Isa held Bruiser in her arms while Dalton's pastor gave the ceremony. It was a good funeral for Bruiser in Jan's back yard.

Isa was kicked out of the Prestwick as her rage was disrupting the very sedate atmosphere. Although her fellow residents were sympathetic with Isa about her dog, she was ready to fight at all times. They couldn't take it. Isa had to go.

Karen showed me a facility with actual cottages where Isa could feel independent but have the support she needed. So, I moved Isa and her belongings, again, to The Villas of Westbrook assisted living facility.

Isa settled down and seemed to accept Dr. Caitlin's diagnosis of multiple sclerosis. I.V. infusions were started. Isa didn't get any of the many frightening side effects we had to sign off on, so we continued with the radical treatment the doctor prescribed.

I bought many loaves of day-old white bread for Isa. She spent all day, every day on her back porch, smoking and throwing bits of bread to the many turtles in the big pond outside her little cottage. At last, she was able to eat real food! She enjoyed the simpler food at the Villas dining room.

More blessings came Isa's way. My friend from the hospice where I volunteered was a masseuse. Jenny offered to massage Isa for free.

I started to see burn marks on Isa's carpet. The nurses showed me burn marks on her mattress too, as if she was falling asleep with a cigarette in her fingers. She was now a fire hazard, a danger to herself and others, but she didn't care. Isa refused to stop smoking inside her little cottage, which was attached motel-style to the other cottages.

I had to do it—her cigarettes had to live at the nurse's station, many yards down a sidewalk and a gravel road in the main building. The nurses would bring Isa a cigarette when they had time to watch her smoke it.

Isa started defiantly dragging her feet in her wheelchair on her way down that gravel road to get a cigarette. She didn't care that she was harming herself. She ripped up her feet so badly, we found ourselves in the ER.

The doctor said Isa was not seriously harmed. It was just surface scratches on her gravel-torn toes. But an unrelated wound was discovered on her ankle that might cause trouble. The doctor shaved off the scab so the wound could heal better, and a vacuum pump was attached to the wound. Isa needed home health to oversee the pump.

Isa started removing the bandages that held the vacuum pump in place then removing the pump from the wound. When nurses found her like this, she swore she didn't do it. She pulled the pump out three times and then the home health nurses refused to treat Isa's wounds. I had to beg.

Isa was violently, viscerally in hate with me for taking her cigarettes away. Of course, she hated me. I got it. It was terrible to have to do that to her. How would we solve this one?

I photographed Isa's living room and bedroom, showing that the carpet and mattress had cigarette burns on them, and then I made a decision. She could not have her own private cottage. The Cottage's director offered Isa a private room in the main building near the screened-in lanai where people could smoke. It was also near the nursing desk. It was a good solution.

## My impossible one

Isa continued her hostility. She was lethal to anyone around her who would not give her a cigarette. She wanted a court date to get rid of me.

Dear Isa,

HERE IS HOW to recover your civil rights:

To regain your rights at a judicial hearing, a minimum of three court-appointed health workers will visit with you; a psychiatrist, medical doctor, and social worker will then present evaluations of your capacity to the court.

From that information, if the judge determines that the client will be able to manage her own affairs competently and safely, rights are restored.

If not, a guardian is appointed to coordinate care and manage affairs (toward the life choices the client would have if she could manage them herself).

For evaluators to recommend competency, the client must demonstrate a sustained pattern of behaviors that show the ability to live successfully and safely. These include:

- Managing one's finances ($3,500 pension) for housing, food, personal expenses, insurance coverage, and health support
- Coordinating proper medical care (general health doctors, therapists and dentists, exercise, and support groups)
- Reliably taking prescribed medications (which are strong narcotics)
- Refraining from actions deemed dangerous (drinking alcohol, smoking while very sleepy, and getting cigarette burns on your carpet and mattress)

With very best regards,
Ann

I found out the professional guardians who were previously approached to accept Isa as their ward were June and Marianne. Their choice was to put Isa in a long-term nursing home, but Dalton couldn't stomach that. Ultimately, it didn't matter— June and Marianne said no to taking on Isa. She was too much trouble.

I tried every possible way to recover Isa. I brought her to a very fine assisted living facility, thinking it would bring out the "lady" in her. I found her a cute cottage, with all services, so she could feel she was living in a real home. I strived to find her real diagnosis.

The fourth time Isa destroyed the vacuum pump and the bandages holding it in place, I placed her in the hospital. Then, I begged and bothered the intake people at the best rehab hospital in Saint Sandton. She had comorbidities, wounds plus M.S. with the need for physical therapy, which qualified her for this very special rehab hospital. I wanted them to evaluate the extent of the damage in her back and legs. She wanted to walk. They accepted Isa for a full MS evaluation.

On the way from the hospital to the rehab hospital, she persuaded the wheelchair bus driver to take a detour to get her cigarettes from the nurse's station at the Villas ALF. When she finally arrived at the rehab hospital, she had a huge fight with the staff about her cigarette carton and then refused to go to her rehab session. She stayed outside in her wheelchair and smoked.

Once Isa started invading other people's rooms, the staff gave up on her. I thought this was Isa's big chance to begin again; she didn't think it was anything at all. She wasn't going to grab any of the lifelines I threw out to her. She was determined to make war.

This was turning into a nightmare. Problems with Isa were all consuming, exhausting and hopeless.

I found another guardian for Isa. Jackie was a tough and seasoned guardian; she promptly accused me of spoiling Isa. (I disagree) Jackie had Isa admitted to a long-term nursing home, where one of the staff said to Isa, "Oh! No! Not you again! I thought I got rid of you when I left the ALF by the river."

I had done all I could for Isa. I didn't want to make the decision to put her in a nursing home. The assisted living facility couldn't take her back. They weren't equipped to care for her wounds, which were not healing due to neuropathy and Isa's refusal to comply with treatment.

For Jackie, it was a no-brainer; for me, it was a very hard decision. It took many months of trying this and trying that, trying to find a way to keep Isa free and safe. A nursing home at forty-two years old! But at least now we knew a lot more about her history. I tried to give her a better quality of life and as much freedom as she could have. It failed. I was unable to recover Isa.

Charlotte, the social worker, reassured me that I had tried everything I could.

I was burnt out by Isa's ten angry phone calls a day. Now I knew more about myself in this calling. I didn't want to simply maintain a ward. I was interested in improving people's lives.

I was not a maintenance person. I was not a guard. I did not believe in having authority or control over another human being. I wanted collaboration. I was creative and ambitious and deeply interested, as long as there was hope of improvement.

Isa was not going to improve. She didn't want to. She was pissed off at everyone in the world because her brother saved her from overdosing.

Is her story typical of the need for guardianship? Yes. To keep her safe from herself and others because she was alive and stuck in a system that couldn't ethically help her end her life.

I had chosen Charlotte to do talk therapy with Isa. Now Charlotte said to me, "Wow! She will be so sorry to lose you!"

Isa soon forgot what I was trying to do for her, with her. She told someone she was glad to get rid of me, that I was a bad guardian. Hey, I might be...

# What I learn from Isabella and her new guardian, Jackie

Recovering from a relentlessly self-destructive soul like Isabella is part of the work for any guardian. These are exactly the kind of souls that belong in guardianship. Years later, Jackie is still Isabella's guardian. Today Isabella lives in the same nursing home. Jackie does not discriminate. She takes the hard cases every time. That's the job. The world needs guardians like her. I had to face that I was limited. I was not that kind of guardian.

Both Charlotte and Amy, an elder lawyer, wanted to give me more cases. I went to meet the people they wanted me to help. I was often able to solve problems in a grey area without guardianship. I got one young man an administrative service that would hold his social security check and pay assisted living for him. It created a safe solution for both the assisted living facility and the resident because social security needed to be sure that their money was used only by the person receiving it and only for that person's needs. He didn't need a guardian. He only needed his money secured. Problem solved.

## Tom

I was working with lawyer Alex M. as power of attorney for a homeless Vietnam veteran named Tom. When he became very ill, he was admitted to the hospital and then a nursing home. Now, Tom was close to death. The nursing home called me because I was a new guardian, and this was an indigent case. More experienced guardians had rosters already too full of indigent cases. I accepted the case and called lawyer Alex M, as is required in overseeing any case. Alex agreed that the best course of action was to create a simple POA (power of attorney).

The staff at the nursing home where he lived had an urgent problem. They couldn't reach Tom's sister, his proxy, the recorded next of kin who was a prostitute and often drunk. There was no "do not resuscitate" order for Tom. So, I went looking for her. I had the number of a garage where her ex-boyfriend worked; he told me she would be at a certain bar. The bartender pointed her out, and I bought her a drink. We talked about her brother and she cried. I had a piece of paper for her to sign. I explained that if we didn't have a signed DNR order, the facility would have to send Tom to the hospital where resuscitation would feel violent and so very cruel on his diminished body. She signed it and asked to see her brother. I took her in my car to visit him. She was very emotional, and he clearly loved her. There were many bedside hugs between them.

Afterwards, at her request, I drove her to a shopping mall. As I drove away, I saw her approach a woman with two kids asking for money. Staff had labeled Tom's sister as dangerous, but I felt Tom's sister needed support. Most guardians don't use their car to drive people around; they have them transported. Not me, I guess. My car was at their service.

Now that the doctor was able to order a DNR, I was able to ask for hospice; they came in and held Tom's hand while I took on the next step of getting him to sign for his own cremation. He had some children by various women who could have signed the papers, but we couldn't find them. If he'd been unable to consent to cremation, we would have had to bury him. He had no money for a coffin. Then we found Tom's older brother in North Carolina, who agreed to the cremation. I had the funeral parlor draw up the papers, which Tom signed. He only had a wee bit of money from social security, which I used to pay the funeral home for cremation, including the cost of sending the ashes to his brother in North Carolina.

I had been a hospice volunteer for years and I continued volunteering after I became a guardian. As a hospice volunteer I was taught how important it was to know what you could and could not do in visits with the dying. I was not comfortable with contagious diseases and this was my prejudice, even as I was trained in precautions. Other volunteers had other difficulties. Most of the time, men normally felt more comfortable holding a vigil beside a dying man. Women felt more comfortable with women in this powerfully intimate setting. Death is intimate. We at hospice always need to be sure that at someone's passing they are not alone. Tom was with one of my fellow volunteers when he passed. I loved hospice for all the ways their big team created painless, peaceful dying and "we are not alone" in that transition.

## A healing circle in every way

In my work as a guardian I knew I was helping people. I felt good. I had Sophie, living with Schizophrenia, Dorothy, abandoned by her daughter hiding in her mother's trailer, and I had just passed Isabella with rage and MS to hard-nosed guardian, Jackie. I was still recovering from the difficult decisions around handing Isabella over to a guardian who was her match, yet the kind of guardian I knew I never wanted to become. And I was struggling with, ashamed of quitting someone and I felt exhausted. My ego was wrapped up in "I'm no quitter". I needed to think of my other clients who were being eclipsed by Isabella C. I needed to form a roster that suited me.

All during this time in guardianship, I was connected with my fellow volunteers at hospice. We met once a month to talk about our hospice cases. We had been learning Reiki and practicing on one another at each meeting. This refreshed me, and I needed refreshing. I also entered the gloriously warm, salty ocean every day, cleansing away the day's difficulties.

This day my Reiki teachers, Nan and Teresa, encouraged me to share with our fellow hospice volunteers about my experiences with Amelia, my "curmudgeon" in the nursing home at Serenity Cove.

I visited Amelia every week for eight months. She was not a curmudgeon, of course. She was lonely and scared. Toward the end, I was her vigil volunteer, so I went much more often, for two hours at a time. I played music and held her hand and answered her questions about when her parents were going to pick her up from school.

"Soon, Amelia. While we wait, tell me what it's like in Ohio in wintertime."

I brought her a soft toy German Shepherd because her dog, a fellow soldier in World War II, was a bomb-sniffing, decorated hero dog. She wanted her real dog. I asked hospice to visit her with a therapy dog

I liked her stories and she reached out to me from her bed when I appeared at her door. Amelia and I held hands on all our visits. We held on tight. And we became close friends. I had great music choices playing most of the time.

I asked her if she liked the music playing.

"Not so much" Amelia said.

"The music sure is helping me!" I told my Reiki circle. They laughed.

I became a hospice volunteer because I was afraid of the moment of death at my father's passing. I did not achieve a graceful presence with my father at that moment. I was awkward, and my voice sounded like it was outside my body when he asked me to sit by him to say goodbye. His death was a few hours away, when I left his hospital room. Fear, discomfort, helplessness, and my expectations about being perfect for this moment helped neither my father nor me.

At 4:00 a.m., I shot bolt upright from my bed and started dressing. My stepmother called as I was dressing. May said my father had died. (I know!) I got to her quickly. We placed the sheet over his head. I was afraid to go into the room after that. It was a shock to see him lifeless.

I became a hospice volunteer to get over that discomfort, because I was not going to be like that when my mother needed me at her time. The orientations, training, and support system at hospice helped me deal with my fear. And now, with Amelia, I wanted to feel differently, and the music helped *me* more than it did Amelia.

I was called at 5:00 a.m. to hurry to her nursing home. Amelia reached out when she saw me. We had only five last minutes, and we were both really glad to be together. We held on tight. When her eyes faded to far, far away, I called to the male nurse who I admired and who was so great with Amelia. He listened to her heart, nodded, and called the doctor in. I

cried. I was so moved to have shared her death. It was, well …
it felt wonderful. It felt like love.

Once a month, six to ten hospice volunteers come together
in a circle to share stories about our dying ones and our feelings
about death. Then we open massage tables and give hands-on to
our fellows: twelve hands hovering over one body, de-stressing,
healing. This was my church.

# CHAPTER FIVE

# The Guardianship
# of Violet P.

Earlier this year, my neighbor Jack, a taxi driver on Westbrook Island, told me that he transported Violet P. to her appointments. Violet lived up the road. She was eighty-nine years old and very difficult; she trusted no one. Jack's daughter, Kerry, had worked for Violet as a personal assistant but had moved away. Now Violet was all alone. Jack asked me to see her; he was worried about her. So, I agreed to find a way to approach her. I wrote a letter to Violet introducing myself.

> Dear Violet,
>
> I moved here to Westbrook Island from New England in November last year. Jack Margate mentioned you to me because he wanted to help you find a new assistant, now that his daughter, Kerry, has moved away. I am an elder advocate and I wonder if you would care to meet with me to see if I could be of service to you.
> My strong points are: Listening. Research. Analyzing options. Managing financial or personal matters with respect and confidentiality. Accompaniment. Advocacy. Care management, which means assistance in finding a good team,

if needed. I have been trained and bonded and sworn to the highest standards of ethics. Sometimes my work requires that I protect a person or their property. Sometimes a person only needs a researcher or someone to speak with in order to make decisions. And once those decisions are made, someone to make it easy to accomplish things. I would be happy to meet with you.

Best regards,
Annie W

To find out how I might approach Violet with my letter, I went to see the bank manager who had been paying Violet's bills.

"Jack Margate asked me to check on Violet," I said. "I want your advice before I do. Are you looking for someone to—"

"She already has guardians." The manager was ice cold.

"Oh, I didn't know. Well then, I'll step away."

A few months later, Jack asked me again about Violet. Could I find out if Violet was being treated well enough? Jack and his wife were concerned that Violet's nursing home might be below the standards she deserved since she could afford the very best.

Jack gave me the name of the nursing home and the telephone number for the guardians. I called and was connected with the lawyer for the guardianship. I explained that Violet's neighbor was concerned about her.

"Yes," she said. "There's some trouble with the case. We're working it out."

"Thank you."

I went to visit Violet. A nurse's companion sat in a chair beside the bed. There was good quality furniture in that small room. I assumed it was from Violet's house.

"I'm Jack's friend," I said to Violet. "He asked me to come see you."

The hospital bed was pretty banged up. It was 11:30 a.m.

"Why are you still in bed this morning?" I asked.

She was very sad. She told me her nephew couldn't save her from being taken over by "them!"

Lawyers constantly warn families and guardians alike that elders can turn against "them" for no reason, no matter how nice and trustworthy they were. I only half believed it.

With Isa, who got a rotten deal in life, there was anger that could not be healed. But with an elder? I always felt there would be a reason for frustration. It might be betrayal, abandonment or fear from being unheard. This would upset and anger the most patient person in the world. Elders in this generation are sensible and forgiving, so when they are pissed off, I look closely, and start asking questions.

A nurse entered with a pill and Violet sat up and eagerly reached for it with frail hands.

"Pain pill," Violet said, "for my arthritis."

The attendant nodded to me and then left the room with the nurse. I was alone with Violet.

Violet wore beautiful pajamas; her tiny, pretty face was pale and her eyes distant.

"Those horrible guardians are taking my money," she said. "My nephew is failing! They told me I could go to court and ask the judge to consider my wishes. They sent a limo for me and we drove a long way, it seemed. Then we ended up at their office, the office of my guardians and their lawyer. I was not at the courthouse, as promised, where I could tell the judge I wanted him to release me, to have control of my own money myself, with people I already trusted. Those horrible guardians told me the judge had to cancel, but that they would take my statement and bring it to him. That riled me up. They wanted to get me all riled up! They lied to me, telling me I could see the judge. I got really upset and couldn't say what I really wanted, and then they filmed me. My attendant came in and drove me back here in her car. No more limousine."

Violet was not out of it. She got right down to business. Was it the whole truth? I didn't know. It was Violet's truth.

What was true? The guardians, June and Marianne, were not able to build trust with Violet. They didn't consider her wishes. They wanted it to look like Violet was crazy.

Violet told me she had tried to bargain with her guardians.

"I'll live in assisted living where I started to feel better again. I won't try to escape, if you'll just set me up there again. I was starting to get out of the wheelchair and have a dance. The attendant was quick, even frightened, that I got out of the wheelchair. I danced several feet without support, but it showed me how much better I was feeling.

"I was out in the parking lot in my wheelchair when several big men surrounded me and took me back inside. I'm not sure I was trying to escape. They were scary men! They said I was trying to escape."

Violet was strong minded, but she was losing hope, checking out. She was very unhappy. She admitted reaching for more and more pain meds, which were given whenever she requested. This disturbed me. Ten years after Uncle Leo's demise, pain meds, Haldol, and all manner of chemical restraints were still helping elders to "behave" or "move on".

# Detective work

I walked into the courthouse and put my coat and briefcase through the screening machines. Then I found the computers dedicated to the court records.

Any member of the public has a right to enter a courthouse and look at public records. Guardians also have the right, through their lawyer during a hearing, to ask a judge to hide records from public view. I found my way into the guardianship/ probate category and entered Violet's full name. So far so good. Violet's records were available.

It turned out that just two days after Jack told me I should go see Violet at her home, an emergency temporary guardianship was declared by June and Marianne, the two guardians in Westbrook. Adult Protective Services was the petitioner; they had offices in the same building as June and Marianne.

I had tried to meet with Adult Protective Services, but they didn't return my calls. Was this their special club I wasn't invited to join? Was this only June and Marianne's territory?

Violet told me she'd started this journey in the emergency room at the local hospital because of bowel difficulty from narcotic pain killers—soon she was in a nursing home. I saw in the court documents that the clerk of the court sent a notice to the nursing home, but Violet didn't receive the notice. The documents were returned to the clerk.

Violet was headed toward emergency temporary guardianship right out of the ER. Was she in urgent danger from neglect, abuse or exploitation? It wasn't stated.

There were many court records for the last five months. Violet had $2.5 million. It was placed with a financial investment firm, and permission was required to access her money. The guardians petitioned the court to pay themselves and the lawyers involved. One lawyer was hired to represent Violet, and another lawyer to represent and run the guardianship. The guardianship petitioned the court for ongoing fees and also to receive $30,000 a month from the arm's-length depository to care for Violet.

Thirty thousand dollars a month! I felt shaken. Later that day I confided in Westbrook lawyer, Owen T. (the lawyer for the guardianship of Isabella C.), and he looked into the case more deeply. He told me that the sale of Violet's house was being disputed by lawyers acting for a nephew. Owen told me that the judge had granted the house sale two days before the allowable time when any member of the public could protest.

It was Christmas time. Maybe everyone had to rush off to a party. Still … it was the same judge who granted $30,000 per month for Violet's care.

I was very uncomfortable. When I sat in his courtroom observing, I had noticed how chummy he was with the guardians and that he favored some lawyers over others. Did he feel sorry for his regular guardians because they had many indigent wards? I couldn't believe a judge was in agreement with $30,000 a month for care. Was I naive?

What budget did the judge approve? I made an educated guess:

| | |
|---|---|
| Nursing home | $240/day x 30 days = $7,200 |
| 24-hour care x $20/hour | $480/day x 30 days = $14,400 |
| Guardian services | $300/week = $1,200. (in the court records) |
| Legal | $2,000/month = $2,000 (in the court records) |
| Restaurant | $1,200/month (because the facility food was bad and Violet could go out with caregivers any time she wanted) |
| **Monthly total** | **$26,000** |

Initially, lawyers make $5,000 to $10,000 per ward for setting the guardianship in motion, but this $2,000 retainer went on for months.

I was sure this financial information was kept hidden from Violet. She certainly felt she had no say in anything at all. Violet had a legal right to collaborate about her money. I was glad to see the records state that her nephew, with lawyers from out of town, challenged the guardianship.

The guardians divided Violet up. Marianne was the guardian of the property, dealing with money and the estate, and June was guardian of the person, dealing with health decisions, and living arrangements. June probably got a deal on 24-hour care attendants (guards) because they came from a home health agency that June created when she was an assisted living administrator. A guardian was not technically supposed to hire their friends and family, but a guardian could have staff. Were they June's staff?

So out of $30,000 a month, $26,000 could add up for care. That left $4,000 for the non-profit company the guardians had created to support their indigent wards.

Robin Hood? Take from the rich and give to the poor? Take from the rich and pay yourselves for your many poor wards? This was an accepted practice? I didn't like it. Was the system at fault? Maybe. Guardianship as a business was not lucrative. Perhaps these guardians effectively strategized within this probably broken system to make a living wage.

I imagined they must have a lot of cases, probably forty to fifty. Owen told me they had over a hundred wards—with seventy-five wards non-paying!

How could anyone manage one hundred wards? I sure didn't like the system. The system didn't respect guardians. Guardians cared, but should they work for free? So, they had to keep taking more and more wards; some wards had to be able to pay them. Just thinking about how no ward got the attention they needed hurt me.

Did I feel sorry for these guardians? Maybe? Like the judge must feel sorry for them?

Nah. There must be some hidden rules of the game. Something was not right.

Something was not ethical. The solid ground on which we must stand had to be ethical practice. Otherwise trust could not happen. We would not be trusted.

The court documents only "suggested" exploitation. Jack told me the guardians accused the nephew from New York of exploiting Violet. They sure were fighting to justify keeping Violet "safe". To protect her from what?

The judge allowed Violet's house to be sold two days before the allotted time for an objection. They knew there was objection from the nephew's lawyer because they were selling the house too cheaply … to a friend. A developer who was buying up houses from little old ladies.

The objection to selling the property came a few days late, but they had the wrong address, so the out-of-town lawyer was trying to petition to get it re-entered correctly for consideration.

I was shocked. I wished I didn't see what I had seen. Owen wasn't pleased either.

He said he would continue to watch the proceedings and asked if I found Violet in an acceptable situation. I told him the room was tiny, but Violet was safe. Maybe too safe. Did she need a twenty-four-hour guard?

I went to see the manager of the bank, again. The manager was distressed.

She told me that June and Marianne tried to enter the safety deposit box room without her presence, and that they looked really rushed and their demeanor was frightened and angry.

"They looked like thieves."

Unbecoming as this behavior was, I understood the two guardians. They didn't trust the manager. They were afraid of her. Really? That is the hardest part of this calling—you suspect everyone. Fear was all around the guardianship of Violet P.

It's the law to have the bank manager present while a guardian inventories the contents of a ward's safety deposit box. The manager, knowing this, stopped them, and because of the animosity between them, she asked a teller to go with the guardians to witness the inventory of Violet's safety deposit box.

June and Marianne expressed strong fear and suspicion of the bank manager. Did they present this to the judge to hasten Violet into an emergency temporary guardianship? Were they paranoid from being guardians too long and from being overworked with one hundred cases? Or were they spreading fear as a strategy to hold onto Violet's money?

I visited the bank manager's boss at the trust department. She confirmed that the manager was trustworthy. She had warned the manager that this was business, not friendship. The bank manager felt uncomfortable, alone, and bitter. Because she cared, she was helping Violet, and now she felt deeply embarrassed. It was hard to shake the feeling of being accused.

I learned that the two guardians threw a net of suspicion over every person involved with Violet: the nephew, the bank manager, Jack, and his daughter. They took every opportunity to declare their suspicion of exploitation, causing each of these people embarrassment and discomfort. These were tools of control. Very damaging. Very isolating for Violet.

The bank manager's boss told me more of the truth about the matter. The bank had a hard time persuading Violet to trust them to keep her money at their trust department and oversee her bills and needs. Violet was saying she regretted not trusting them, because now she was trapped. The guardians had taken charge of all her money.

"Help me!" she'd said.

I visited Violet a second time. She told me the things she needed. Her hearing aid was broken. The arm of her wheelchair was lopsided and uncomfortable. She needed new glasses. She told me her friend at the bank had been accused of exploiting her. She said if she could see her checkbook, she could prove it wasn't true. She told me that she had wanted to give her grand-nephew money so her sister wouldn't want for anything, but he said it wasn't needed. Now she wished she'd given him the money so at least that money would be safe from 'them'.

The guardians knew I was with Violet and interrupted me. They called my cell and asked me to meet them at their lawyer's office.

This was not the first time I'd met them. A while back, I

had seen them in an assisted living facility parking lot where we both had wards and I introduced myself.

"What are you?" they asked, laughing at me. "An actress?" They were nasty and sarcastic. I guess that short year as an actress could be seen on the internet. They had no idea I was a producer responsible for delivering movies on time and on budget.

I knew being a guardian could be dangerous; rescuing people from abuse, neglect and exploitation, was a job for heavyweights. I was not afraid of responsibility.

I, however, was unprepared for the brutal, competitive, territorial way in which this particular guardianship business operated. They thought actresses were dumb? They were blatantly insulting me. They didn't know I was a very good detective, and like most actresses, a keen intuit of character. They didn't know I had looked into their court records.

Now I wanted to know how much they would tell me. I wanted to discuss the outrageous amount of Violet's expenses, but I wasn't going to be the one to bring it up. I was curious to know what they would tell me about the money. I entered the boardroom and sat down with the two guardians and their lawyer.

The lawyer accused me of having a lack of integrity.

"This is a protected person and you, as a guardian, should know that."

"To my mind, none of us are above scrutiny," I said. "Violet has asked to go back to assisted living where she can go on outings and eat great food, and you can still keep the guards around her, I guess. Why a nursing home?"

They didn't answer.

I thought perhaps they were right. I might have called them first to ask permission to visit Violet. I had phoned this lawyer to say I had heard from a neighbor that they were concerned about Violet. I had phoned Owen to see how I should proceed. He was cool with an unannounced visit to Violet.

Now they said, "Why doesn't the neighbor go see her himself?"

I didn't say what I was thinking: "Because he is afraid! Because you've accused every person who could visit Violet of exploitation. Because there's fear all around this case!"

I suddenly felt I might be in danger, being at the meeting without *my* lawyer. I felt vulnerable, and all my words left me. I had become the dumb actress they thought I was! Silence prevailed for several seconds. An eternity.

"We don't see any neighbors bringing her a pie," Marianne said.

"Yes," I said. "Good idea."

I believed Violet was being purposely isolated, which is an indicator of abuse. The guardians finished our meeting by forbidding me to ever see Violet again. And then they asked, "Are you going to continue with your guardianship business?"

I felt their sub-text: "Because if you do, we're going to destroy you." I felt they were threatening me. Did they know I saw what I wished I didn't see in the court records?

"I am not sure I will continue as a guardian," I said. "I'm not sure I agree with guardianship practice as it stands today. Please consider helping Violet back to assisted living where she can improve, with good quality food and quality of life standards."

I didn't feel comfortable with what I had done, and I couldn't go anywhere with it. I was forbidden to see her. Violet was able to call on the phone. She called me; I had no route to her. I reassured Violet that Kerry, her former assistant, said she would visit her soon. I couldn't help but think that, if Jack's daughter, Kerry, had replaced herself before she took off, Violet would be free today.

## Does it start in the ER department?

The most vulnerable elder in this society is Violet: a widow with money living alone. This widow is feisty, determined, mistrustful, and frightened that she's losing it. She is headed for a crisis—a pain crisis and then a bowel crisis from the opiate meds prescribed for the pain.

Then, Violet is all alone in the emergency room for the second time in a month. More often than we realize she is vulnerable to imprisonment and financial harvesting by the very system that's in place to help and protect her.

The weary folk inside that system see her as a pain in the ass, falling into dementia, becoming a "she," talked about, unheard, as she calls out louder and louder, "I'm here! Right in front of you! You can talk to me directly. I'm telling you. I want to stay in my home. Don't do this to me! I want to go home!"

But they aren't listening. They're not thinking, "How can this elder get what she wants?" They're afraid of how much energy she'll require. How much time. How much money do elders cost in their hospital budget? Lots!

Someone in the ER is afraid of her or for her and calls the guardians. Then the guardians call Adult Protective Services.

But wait a minute! Violet was recoverable. She had a bowel blockage. She needed some extra help at home, but no, no one was standing beside her in the ER holding her hand saying exactly that. Advocating. Why was this elder all alone in a hospital?

The Adult Protective Services investigators instigated this proceeding out of the ER at the hospital. That was very fast. Why? They were starting to frighten me.

Was I really sure I was seeing this correctly? Maybe I didn't understand what being a guardian was. Could I not see the "guard" in guardian? No elder should be alone at a hospital.

Owen decided to watch Violet's case but not act. He advised

me, because I had just one case with this judge, to lay low. My business was in its infancy, therefore vulnerable.

I couldn't accuse the guardians of inappropriate actions without them making good on their threats. I knew they were determined to boot me out of their territory. I couldn't confront the judge about agreeing to $30,000 a month or for being fooled into imprisoning a widow for her money.

What if I was wrong? No wonder this widow found it hard to trust anyone—so did I.

I had seen how I protected Sophie from herself. She knew she needed a guardian. But elders have different problems than a ward with mental illness. They all seemed to have a broken heart or deep loneliness. But was there a distinction about who should be a ward and who should not be a ward? I didn't agree with Sophie losing her civil rights either. She wanted to vote. I petitioned the court to reinstate her civil right to vote. She was very intelligent. She had studied the candidates better than anyone I knew. The court granted it. It seemed that elders lost their civil rights only because they had become old.

Many of these elders can improve and, very importantly, retain their rights. It seemed too convenient that they're hurried into guardianship. They are declared incapacitated, and they lose their civil rights, a cruel destiny for an elder.

No. I didn't like it. I didn't agree with it. Civil rights were not confiscated in Germany. They dared not after the 1930s and '40s destruction of thousands of beautiful people deemed less than desirable. I felt no vulnerable person should lose their civil rights. I mentioned this idea to my fellow guardians at a networking meeting.

"If we don't have authority over them," they said, "how can we get things done?"

It's true. Part of a guardian's job is to take control of things in a crisis. I still did not think they needed to control a vulnerable person. I listened and collaborated with my wards, but it took time. I was looking to heal them. I felt I couldn't serve more than five wards at a time. That was full time for me. No guardian could make a living with five wards at a time. So, my business model was ridiculous. But if guardianship as my calling was about advocacy, and righting the ship, healing and life enhancement, I was managing just fine?

Running a business? Oh dear. This is a story that proves why guardians should not have independent businesses. Guardians must be paid at arm's-length for their work in collaborating with their wards without the hard mess of running an independent business too. There could not have been enough time in a month to care for so many wards. Time was a big problem, and wards suffered from neglect because of the time challenges guardians faced every day. I heard in our meetings how wrenching it was to choose one ward in need over another.

Violet's money might have needed protecting, but was it being protected now? The two guardians who financially harvested Violet were created by the system. They showed me how impossible it was to do this independent business model called guardianship. They had acquired over one hundred wards, and three quarters of them were indigent and couldn't pay. Somehow two people had to address the problems of all one hundred, and with meager earnings. So, they created the Robin Hood effect. Rob the rich to keep the business going, so they could continue to serve the poor. They adapted to their system.

Essentially, they did a job, but it wasn't my style. Not what I wanted for any elder. This is what leads me to believe that guardians should be salaried by the state at arm's- length and not survive by keeping a wealthy widow inside guardianship for her money. It cannot justify the good those guardians do for their many indigent wards. The system is broken.

I didn't check on Violet again. I relayed the guardians' message to Jack. "Why don't you visit Violet, yourself? Bring her a pie."

"Oh no, we don't want to see Violet," Jack said. "We just want to know where she disappeared to and how all her money could be taken from her, because we're scared it could happen to us."

Oh no! Jack would never have stood up for Violet in a court of law. I realized that people didn't care as much as I thought they did.

I consulted with my mentor guardian, Mary.

"Your neighbor Jack used you," Mary said. "Be careful. Maybe you could have figured out his motive was selfish sooner. He may have put you in harm's way."

I told Mary I felt Violet shouldn't be in a nursing home. Mary informed me that the nursing home had a good reputation and so did the guardians.

I had seen my mentor guardian be tough and tender. I respected her. Now she sounded as if an awful lot of these situations slid right off her back. She had an air of forgiveness about her and she included me in that forgiveness.

"Try to forgive June and Marianne. They probably think you were trying to steal her from them."

"I never thought about that." I pondered. "I was checking on Violet's degree of wellbeing for a friend. Actually, I thought *they* were stealing, or the system forced them to take Violet's money against her wishes. What's that called?"

"I agree," Mary said. "It's uncomfortable sometimes, but that's the deal. Take it or leave it."

I felt more grounded by Mary, but I would never agree to be paid by holding an elder in a nursing home against her will for her money. I said to myself, "Be careful, be cautious, be prudent. Have objectivity. You can't help Violet. Consider your other wards." I fired back at myself, "But it's not fair! Something is terribly wrong here!" I still mourn Violet's circumstance today. I cannot get over it.

# Honoring Violet

This is what Violet did for me and for her neighbors, who were very frightened that control of their lives could be taken from them just because they were old and fragile and had money.

I started to give talks and offer advice to elders on how to avoid guardianship. How to prepare for the day when you might need support. How to find care managers and develop trust with professionals of your own choosing before you actually need them. How to set it up legally, including a lawyer and doctor who know you well and how to create a living will that's very specific. A list of people you trust and want in your life. A list of people you may have reason not to trust at some point. And as things change, keeping these things up to date. A will and pre-need funeral planning. The trust department in the bank that you know. Let time test out all these connections.

If there is a crisis brewing, call a certified geriatric care manager. While it might cost a few thousand dollars to receive this support, guardianship is more expensive in every way, costing at least $10,000 to set up, and costing emotionally. Once a person is declared incapacitated, it is very difficult in this court system to reverse. So, until we can fix that discrepancy mandated in our law and practice, avoid guardianship.

I explained "voluntary guardianship," the only kind I believe in for elders. This keeps the elder in charge, the way their wisdom mandates, even as they become too fragile to manage their affairs alone. The guardian *must* listen and collaborate because the elder has the authority to fire them.

## The Voluntary Guardianship of Agnes M.

Eighty-seven-year-old Agnes was beautiful in every way. The parish nurse, my friend Abby, asked me to meet with Agnes and her two daughters from out of town.

Agnes was fed up with her local daughter, Fern. She couldn't stop Fern from barging into her house, yelling at her, and grabbing her credit card or ATM card, insisting she was going shopping for her mum.

A later study of the bank transactions showed that Fern mostly went to the movies and bought fast food and wine. Fern also took a trip to Colorado with her mother's credit card, and while she was gone, Agnes became ill with a urinary tract infection that led to sepsis. Agnes almost died. That was when Agnes's out-of-town daughters, Hanna and Rachel, stepped in.

Agnes had a very clear idea of what she wanted. She asked me to say "no" to her local daughter, for her. I said I would. Agnes was a great mum to all her girls and wise. She knew she needed an arm's-length trusted one.

Agnes, Hanna, Rachel, and I met with lawyer, Amy P. We proceeded with Amy to remove Fern from the power of attorney. Agnes signed a revoking document that I took to the bank, removing Fern's authority. Agnes was added to my roster in a voluntary guardianship, a glorified power of attorney, with the court overseeing and holding me accountable. Agnes retained all her civil rights; she could also fire me if she wasn't pleased with my work. Instead she hugged me and mothered me too! What a darling!

While the paperwork to the court would take three to four weeks, Amy suggested I pretend I already had the authority to say "no" to the local daughter.

Agnes and her roommate, Nora, were afraid. I changed the locks on the house. I instructed the "good" daughters to help Agnes at the bank by canceling the credit cards and ATM cards. I was not as yet authorized to help at the bank. Agnes and I hid the checkbook. Fern could no longer barge in and take money and credit cards whenever she wanted.

Then I met Fern, Agnes's abusing daughter, at Starbucks. I bought us a coffee. I took a deep breath. I explained that I would be taking over the business affairs for her mother. Fern let me know she'd been doing a great job taking care of her mum for years now. She didn't mention the entitlements that she'd helped herself to. I asked her to find another way to "earn" money, now that I would be taking over the care for Agnes.

It was tense for a week. Nora acted as a buffer for the new phone calls coming from the furious, embarrassed daughter. Her eighty-seven-year-old sweetheart of a mother was able to say that I was her guardian and that I was the bad guy. Fern stopped taking money from her mother. Fern also stopped talking to her mother and sisters for a year.

Agnes wanted to move into assisted living at The Oaks. I helped with that transition. Now, I had both Dorothy and Agnes there.

After a year of not speaking to her mother, Fern got a job and started visiting her mother again, for love reasons. Good for her!

## Going home

I had been a guardian for over a year. I took a holiday, and my fellow new guardian, Melanie, was kind enough to officially be temporary legal guardian for Sophie. My good friend Abby, the parish nurse, agreed to watch over Agnes and Dorothy.

I spent two months at my mum's house up north. My own loved ones had not seen me in a year. I figured my apprenticeship was over. Did I want to continue? My mother was ninety. My step father, ninety-four, was living with dementia and even though they had a fulltime caregiver from heaven, I still had a lot of tasks to perform to secure their future. I prepared their taxes, coordinated extra support for them and arranged to be the person to contact in case of an emergency. I was one of five children and our family gathered at our parents' this summer. We painted their house. We cooked mum's favorite recipes. (She had become legally blind) We barbecued, swam in the cove, danced on the deck. We toasted our gratitude. We were fortunate to be well, to love one another: we were relatively carefree for now and we knew it. We shared a good time that summer.

## Returning to advocacy

I thought I had paved a way to continuing as a guardian. I had to recover from the real exhaustion that came from a client like Isabella, who would have killed me, not because of who she was, but because of the kind of guardianship I was delivering. I was caring, an empathetic life force as an advocate. I was a believer in freedom at almost any turn in the road. I worked hard to keep my people as free as they could be. I was a good and ambitious care manager, heading off crisis. I could find solutions, and this was successful for Sophie, Dorothy, and Agnes, with whom I had the right balance of caring and objectivity.

When I returned to the south, I attended a networking luncheon. Roy, my friend and fellow new guardian, corralled me. June and Marianne told him I was burnt out and I wasn't taking any cases. Really? Oh! I forgot. An adult protective investigator *had* called me to insist that I take a case. She was unfriendly from the beginning of the call, and then she was testy, even hostile when I said I would be away for another month, so I could not take the case.

I had certainly needed to step back and rest and examine how I could be a good guardian. Roy was disturbed by June and Marianne. He told me they didn't like me one bit, and I should be careful. I wasn't surprised. Now I knew for sure I had reason to be afraid of June and Marianne. I had stepped on their toes and I seemed to be a little mosquito to them, easily squashable. Now I knew they had begun squashing me.

If there was not $2.5 million available to feed June and Marianne's struggling business, I believe Violet's care would have been very different. No twenty-four-hour guard disguised as care attendant. Perhaps no guardianship at all. Violet didn't feel she needed protecting from anyone when she was plucked from her nest. It burned me all right.

I could not abide that Violet had been made to look crazy and then filmed and officially presented to serve a guardianship enterprise. I saw Violet as sane and justifiably angry. To listen to Violet's wishes was the least they could have done. I now saw the paradox that to creatively solve problems took time most guardians could not afford to give. If a guardian had a decent fee for each case, whether the person was indigent or wealthy, this would be a solution for all concerned. People would not accuse guardians, as I do now, of financially harvesting the rich.

June and Marianne's business and care strategies were heartbreaking to me. I wasn't sure I really understood guardianship as the noble profession I thought it was. I wasn't sure I would continue to be a guardian if I had to enter their world. I didn't like them at all.

Philippa, a care manager who worked with these two guardians, told me they were capable of throwing a snake on my back if I did anything to disturb them.

Gulp, I had already done something to disturb them!

## The grey area before guardianship

I investigated a case for my friend, MSW Charlotte. A woman in talk therapy with Charlotte was allegedly being exploited by her husband and son. The son had power of attorney for his parents, who were both severely mentally ill.

The parents asked me to get them a lawyer so they could get the power of attorney revoked.

I studied the family history. The court history was long. I looked at the status of the house and cars. I met or spoke on the phone with friends, doctors, and therapists. The parents had just moved to The Villas of Westbrook, which both Charlotte and I liked. The son was now fixing up their old house ten minutes away. The nutritional needs of the mother had not been met previously by the son, as he, at 23, went to school and had a small cell phone repair business. This situation was difficult for him. He neglected her, but not intentionally. He simply couldn't cope with the situation. Now, at the ALF, his mother was having three meals a day.

With legal advice, the status quo was not changed. The family was afraid of guardianship and the son wanted to do right by his parents. The son was frustrated and stressed by too much responsibility. The administrator at the Villas ALF and I helped the family to de-stress.

By educating the son on the ethical and legally safe way to protect his parents, I was able to set him straight on being careful not to abuse the power of attorney. There is no "power" in a power of attorney—only responsibility for helping someone with their wishes as long as the wishes do no harm.

The assisted living facility was made representative payee to protect his mother's social security from her husband, and the son paid the rest. This situation might benefit from a guardian; however, during the month I investigated, I was able to see that the parents needed to control their spending. His mother was a serious shopaholic. His father leaned on his mother for money every chance he got. It turned out the son was doing a fairly good job of controlling this for their safety and security, and I hoped he would get the support he needed to continue caring for his parents.

Charlotte felt secure about the choice to stay with the status quo and ramped up her support of the whole family. Charlotte was a cool social worker; she helped a lot of people. I was lucky to be working with her.

## What I learned because of my work with Charlotte

Independent social workers who also practice talk therapy in any community are a hidden treasure. Find them. Pay them. For your information, straight Medicare (not an advantage plan) pays for working with a social worker, if you are over sixty-five or disabled. Social workers will ease your pain. Many are psychotherapists. They will also get you the services you need. They will apply for Medicaid waiver programs if you cannot afford to go into assisted living. They will point you to a good guardian if exploitation is suspected. Independent social workers like Charlotte can be found in your community.

# CHAPTER SIX

# The Self-Determination of Maddy M.

The community of Westbrook Island was buzzing with gossip. A bookkeeper had absconded with thousands of dollars from the golf club. It was embarrassing for this community of retired executives who forgot to watch the books on their own private club. And then there was more gossip when Violet, an elder from the Christ Church choir seemed to disappear into guardianship. She was removed from the island and placed in a nursing home, and her money and property were seized. People were frightened that scoundrels were coming to town and stealing money right out from under their noses. Did Violet have to be plucked from her nest?

The feeling was that, as we age, control of our lives could be taken away and placed in the hands of strangers. Even if the strangers were court supervised, it felt wrong—as if the wrong person was in jail. The victim of the crime was in captivity, rather than the perpetrator. The pastor asked, "Why can't people leave our elders alone?" The community was tense. I became sensitive to the fact that 'Guardian' was a dirty word around here. I started calling myself an advocate. It felt truer about me.

I saw a classified advertisement in the little island newspaper.

A part-time personal assistant was needed. This could provide a little money to help support my advocacy business while it developed. I called and met with Sarah Kinder and Maddy Moss at Sarah's apartment.

Maddy was hard of hearing, I pulled my chair up close to where she was sitting on the couch. I started asking Maddy questions so I could understand what might be needed.

"What are your wishes for a collaboration like this?"

"Well how much do you cost?"

"If it's errands and driving and groceries," I said, "it could be $15 an hour. If it's care management, bill paying, and administration, it could be a little more, depending on what you can afford. I'll tell you what. We could work together for a week and see if we get along, and then we could decide what to do at that time. It will be fair. I can say that."

Maddy was charming. We comfortably fell into conversation and I learned she had golfed all her life, six times a week. Her husband, Harry, had died five years ago.

Sarah spoke of how things were done around here by neighbors. But now Maddy wanted to choose her own team.

"Maddy has a leg that's a bit lazy," Sarah said. Otherwise, Maddy seemed robust; she was eighty-nine years old.

Maddy leaned over and whispered to me, "I have a little dementia," but I didn't see that at this meeting.

Sarah explained that she had worked with Maddy all summer, but Maddy had been losing hope and was depressed. Maddy smiled and reached for Sarah's hand.

"I'm better now. Sarah has helped me pull myself together."

"I found Maddy on her front balcony swatting mosquitoes off her neck," Sarah said. "She was sitting on a kitchen chair. It looked like a slum. Most people on this island have a lanai."

"Yes," Maddy said. "I sat outside thinking many days, many sunsets, what am I going to do? What am I going to do? And then I saw a rainbow, and I thought something good will come today. And here it is! A someone! Sarah!"

"I took Maddy swimming at the better pool near my mum's condo in this same complex. We had fun."

"I needed exercise," Maddy added.

Now, Sarah had a new job at the town clerk's office and could no longer manage her mother's needs or Maddy's. She further explained that Maddy simply had a little disorientation at night. She was clear to work with and able to manage her bills, but an administrative assistant could help out on that chore too. The condo was rented to Maddy by the Picards. The landlords were Maddy and Harry's golfing buddies of twenty-five years.

Two days later, on Friday, I got a call from Sarah. Maddy liked me best, but she was worried she couldn't afford me. It would be about twelve hours of work a week.

"Okay," I said, "let's see what's needed. I'll work for $12 an hour for the week and then we can talk again. She's right in my back yard."

I emailed my favorite local elder lawyer, Owen T., and asked, "Because I am a certified guardian, would it be wise to have a contract to work as a straight personal assistant for someone?" He thought something drawn up simply between the parties would do. I told him we would try it out for a week before deciding on a real arrangement.

On Saturday night, I was enjoying a cruise in my neighbor's boat for cocktails and a gorgeous sunset when I got a call from Sarah.

"Maddy's crying. Could you come over tonight? I don't think she's eaten dinner."

I found Maddy sitting in the dark staring at her front door, which was wide open. When I appeared, she was startled, but when she saw it was me, she relaxed. I turned on the kitchen lights. I had brought ingredients with me on my bike: eggs, butter, bread. I walked to her chair, kneeled down, and shook her hand.

"Hi," I said. "How about some scrambled eggs?"

"Okay."

I saw her apartment for the first time. It was adequate. I found a frying pan and put it on the burner. It started to smoke immediately. The pan was smeared with old grease. I started again. I took another pan, washed it, and made eggs.

Maddy was still sitting in the chair staring at the door.

"Come to the table." I smiled at her.

She came and sat down. I served her, and she seemed okay now. She ate it all up.

I started to question her about food. She told me cookies and Coca-Cola kept her going. I decided to make some very good food in the next few days.

On Sunday morning, Sarah called at 8:30 a.m. and asked me to meet her at Maddy's.

"Maddy's in a lot of pain … sharp, stabbing leg pain." The three of us decided together we'd better go to the ER.

Because Maddy was on the second floor and couldn't walk down her stairs, I called the island ambulance, by the regular phone number, not 911. I asked the ambulance to come quietly. They complied. A police car came too. The policemen stayed in their car in the parking lot. Sarah told me one of the policemen was the landlord's son.

Two nice attendants from Westbrook Fire Station carried Maddy down the condo stairs. Maybe living on the second floor wasn't going to work anymore.

In the ER at the hospital, an X-ray was ordered. I had

thought I was going to be doing a few errands, pay bills, make better food, and have fun with Maddy, who I liked very much. I didn't expect to be in the ER with her. While we waited, I started asking questions; Maddy seemed eager to tell me about her life.

This is her story:

Maddy and Harry had a honeymoon of a life. No kids. She was a long-time human resources manager at a Fortune 500 company. She hired and fired people. She was fair-minded. She became a person to be respected. Maddy had power.

"But I didn't flaunt it." She smiled at me, almost shy.

When they weren't working, she and Harry, a vice-president at the same company, played golf. Maddy never cooked because her mother would cook dinner for her and Harry every night. Harry and Maddy did great barbeques on the weekend, but really, they had little responsibility in caring for themselves. Life was great.

They traveled all over the world playing golf; Maddy was a great golfer. When they came to this tiny seaside community for the winter, they joined the golf club, which turned out to be a whole little society within the more tourist-oriented Westbrook Island. It was "Mayberry" and the golf club, laughably small, was indeed the social hill to climb. Maddy didn't care about that hill. She was looking for a good golf game. Harry felt differently.

Harry loved coaching the "gals" and those gals thought his lessons were the greatest.

Maddy didn't mind. She was secure in herself and sensible about her relationships. She trusted herself. From years of hiring and firing human beings, she was a good judge of character. She would know if Harry fell out of love with her.

"And Harry always came home." She smiled. I felt she must have been a fine manager, indeed.

As they got older, they traveled less and lived between a camp in Vermont which they owned and this sunny little spot they rented each winter. There were twenty-six golf courses within a fifteen-mile radius. They were not fancy types; however, they sure did land in a community where fancy people lived. The Picards were fancy. Maddy took it in stride. Just because Mrs. Picard was impressed with herself, her influence, and her money, it didn't mean she was a good golfer. The husbands were a good match for the game, and Maddy Moss put up with Betty Picard because of that.

It was when Harry was on his way out that he made legal arrangements with his golfer friend, Jerry Picard, to take care of Maddy after he was gone.

"That got my dander up!" Maddy said.

Had her husband forgotten how successful she was at managing things at the company where they both worked? She wanted to manage her own affairs and choose her own collaborators. But it was hard to refuse to sign things when the love of her life was dying and wanted to know his good friend, Jerry, would watch out for her. So Maddy signed the papers to reassure her darling.

Harry died and Maddy got into the Irish whiskey pretty good for a few years. Harry's golfing buddies, although they considered Maddy beneath them, tried their best to include her. After all, Harry had paid for that by having Maddy sign a will leaving all their money to the Picards.

So, Harry paid in advance for Jerry to watch over his wife. He minimized Maddy at his death by having papers drawn without discussing it with her first, and now she was pissed off about it.

"Why did I sign those papers, anyway?" It was his dying wish? Because it made him happy? Maddy was no sissy or wallflower. She was feisty and independent—except maybe where Harry was concerned.

Maddy saw that Betty was the one in charge in the Picard household; Jerry was a little afraid of his wife. Betty considered Jerry one of the children and he adored her. Beautiful, brilliant, influential, and loving it, Betty put them on the society map, while Jerry collected rents from properties that had been in his family for a long time. They were very rich because of it.

Maddy and Harry did very well for themselves in life too. They had investments and great pensions, but now Maddy wasn't sure she had control of her money. She wanted control, but the Picards had her sign her bank accounts over to them so they could pay her bills for her.

"Why did I do that?" she asked. "I want to get away from them."

While Maddy cried for two years after Harry died, Jerry rented her one of their condos; it wasn't a very nice one, but she didn't complain. She went to the tiny golf club for lunch most days and Betty often had lunch with her. Maddy was embarrassing because she cried often; she couldn't hold it back.

Betty would walk through the club with Maddy, apologizing for her.

"See," she would say, "she won't stop crying. She just won't stop crying."

This was so humiliating that Maddy stopped going to the club.

Maddy hoped Betty meant to do right by her. "After all," she said, "I'm the reason all Betty's five kids will be assured of prosperity in the future. I really don't mind that. But I also know Betty would not have been upset if I'd died of a broken heart a month after Harry."

Betty was frustrated and impatient with Maddy. She'd say, "What do you want? I've called you every day for five years. I invite you all the time to watch the kids swim in the pool and you don't want to."

"I didn't want those calls either!" Maddy answered. "We were both faking it. She and I only pretended to be friends. I think Jerry cares about me, but he can't help me. He can't do what he promised Harry."

Maddy had other friends she cared for in this small "Mayberry" town with a golf club essentially run by queen bee Betty.

Betty knew her way around celebrity golf tournaments; she was a high-society person. Maddy was a truly great golfer; she had played with celebrities all over the world.

"Betty has everyone on a string," Maddy said rolling her eyes. "I held onto the friendship because I saw what deep friends Harry and Jerry were. Now, I see the pain in the back of Jerry's eyes about breaking his promise to Harry. He promised to include me, care about me, and help me manage my affairs when I needed it. That time could be now."

"I could trust Jerry, but Betty took over, lest he screw it up. Betty is so impatient and glamorous and bossy. I see that Jerry watches the heaviness of that on me. He feels that way himself. He would never go against his wife. There would be hell to pay."

Jerry knew how precious Maddy was to Harry. How much the friendship must have meant to Harry for him to ask Jerry to watch out for her, and Harry paid for it in such a generous way. Jerry liked Maddy too. She told good jokes. He liked her New England style and no-nonsense wisdom. She was fair-minded.

"I was one of the guys. My Harry didn't know that Jerry was not the one in charge of things. Wasn't Betty a very pretty

flirt, adequate golfer and doting mother? Harry had it wrong."
Maddy knew who Betty was.

"Betty relished influencing things. She developed a spy
system and if someone didn't like her influence, well then, she
didn't like them. They couldn't be in her club. I've watched
these dynamics for years."

Betty called each and every one of her five children every
day. The children were beloved and each one knew not to
dislike the calls. They were a small price to pay for having
mom on their side. She was very successful for them: the right
schools, the right friends, the right husbands and wives. They
all stayed in "Mayberry," but one. Maddy saw Betty cut the girl
off. That child was punished for leaving.

Now Betty called Maddy every day too. For the past five
years! Maddy didn't like Betty's daily calls. Sure, Betty knew
Maddy was beneath her. Maybe everyone was beneath Betty
Picard. Maybe that was it. Betty never invited Maddy to
church with them. Maddy stayed a few pews back with other
friends, and that was okay with her. The pastor knew Betty and
Jerry very well. They gave a lot, even by attending his church.
Prestigious parishioners, they were great citizens and donated
to their town projects and to their church. Nobody really knew
about their financial ties with Maddy. Maybe a few golf club
members knew. And it was Betty's club, after all.

After two years, Maddy hung up her pity party and got on
with life. She played golf once more. Maddy traveled to her camp
in Vermont often.

"My friends up there are few, but they are more dear to me."

She felt the stirrings of forgetfulness and wished her husband were there to hold her hand because she had so few people, she could ask to hold her hand. She admitted she needed a little help now. Her friends in Vermont were busy with their children and troubled with one illness after another.

Maddy's sister, now dead, had lived with a woman all her life, and although it wasn't talked about in those days, Maddy liked her and liked them as a couple. Her sister's partner was a good choice for Maddy in talking things out, but they had lost touch.

"Do you want me to try and find your sister's partner?" I asked.

"I'm not sure she would care. I thought to move back up to Vermont and find senior living for myself up there, but then my aches and pains started to get the better of me. The warm weather helped, even though the furniture didn't. I would never stoop to ask for anything from Betty and Jerry. They're my landlords and I can't even tell them the furniture in their apartment is uncomfortable. The bed is hard, and I found myself moving cushions on the couch around to try to sculpt a good nest where I could cuddle for a decent night's sleep. How can I collaborate with them on my financial affairs if I can't even ask them to help me improve the furniture?"

Maddy had her pride. She was pissed off at Harry for putting Jerry in charge and pissed off at Jerry for cowering beneath Betty's gaze. Maddy made it clear she didn't want Betty interfering in her life.

"Dr. Dunn told the Picards I had dementia."

"What do you think about that, Maddy?" I asked.

"I'm afraid I might have a little dementia. I'm thinking it over. I couldn't say what I really wanted in that examining room where my doctor suddenly got mean, like it was a big chore to be near me."

"Dr. Dunn seemed impatient. He was mad at me. The tests were memory tests and other tests to see if I was nuts or not, and I got really mad and acted nuts, you know, in a sarcastic way to say, 'Here it is! Here is nuts! Is this what you think you will see?' I got really angry and they all looked really scared.

"Then I got more mad, furious! I couldn't think, so I argued badly and cried and I really did act crazy. I trusted no one in the room. I demanded a new doctor.

"Betty acted hurt, like she was my best friend. How dare I tell her doctor, her friend, that she wasn't my best friend. Damn! The doctor was comforting Betty! What about me? I sure could have used a little comforting."

So, there was an attempt to test Maddy at Dr. Dunn's office. Maddy walked out on impatient, aggressive behavior by the doctor, and Dr. Dunn didn't know it was probably arthritis with no sleep, malnutrition, and depression. Was the doctor frustrated, short on time? Did he want to please Betty

Picard, the one in charge. Betty wanted a dementia diagnosis. It seemed convenient to call it "dementia" and prove it by getting the elder all riled up before testing. Was this a pattern I was seeing? I was worried about hearing that this sick strategy existed.

Maddy could not make her wishes known to them that day. She could say what she wanted of Betty and Jerry now in the ER. She was rehearsing on me.

"Betty and Jerry, I want you to be my acquaintances, and you can have the money. I won't change the will, but please allow me to find the people who actually want me to live well and will be kind enough to help me a little in life the way I wish. After I die, you can have control. I would prefer to choose my collaborators, like Sarah, while I'm still alive."

Maddy had acted up instead. She felt very frightened. She was torn up about where to begin to unravel this mess. She knew she would self-sabotage. A part of her said, "Okay just kill me now. Put me out of my misery."

Shame-faced, Maddy said, "I was out of control. I was angry. I taunted them with gibberish"

And there they were, still whispering to each other:

"Oh dear, then it is dementia with paranoia," the doctor whispered.

"She needs a specialist, does she?" Betty asked.

"I'm in the room! Talk to me!" Maddy demanded. She fired a look at Jerry. "Stand up for me! You promised my Harry you would!" But Jerry remained silent.

Maddy made a stab at self-advocacy. "I refuse to see a psychiatrist who'll say I'm nuts and lock me up."

She was so angry, so very angry. She didn't believe one person in the room cared about her wishes or her wellbeing. Maybe one ... maybe Jerry. But he wouldn't lift a finger, and his shame kept him down. His wife adored him. He didn't dare rock the boat because he'd be the one who would drown.

The ER doctor came back to Maddy and me. He gave Maddy a cortisone injection in her left bursa and reassured her that she didn't have a fracture. The hospital felt okay to me that day.

I took Maddy home in my car and picked up her prescription for anti-inflammatory pills ($3.20) and Boost ($8.49). We went very slowly up the stairs to her apartment. I filled pill boxes with instructions on paper created by Sarah. I gave the anti-inflammatory pills to Maddy with a liverwurst sandwich. It was a blessing that Sarah had bought liverwurst. Maddy's fridge had cookies, Coca-Cola, and take-out salad, which needed to be thrown out. Maddy was worried about having enough money to live. She said she went out to the golf club for lunch but worried about that cost.

"What do you have for lunch?"

"A bowl of chili, usually."

The next day, I canceled my meetings and stayed with Maddy all day. I didn't usually do personal care, but she was injured, so I helped her in and out of the shower. Her bed was very hard. It felt to me like the sheet couldn't hide a cheap mattress. I noted that a mattress pad of memory foam could be purchased.

I made Jacques Pepin's yummy apple pancake in my iron skillet at her house. I did laundry, and we managed to make it down the stairs to a first appointment with a new doctor, Dr. Carrington. Now in the doctor's waiting room, Maddy smiled.

"I stood strong. Now, I finally have my appointment with Dr. Carrington."

"Good," I said, smiling too.

"They are returning tomorrow from their summer place up north. I want my own doctor in place before Betty can object."

Maddy was still in very bad pain. Dr. Carrington arrived and looking at the report from the ER, suggested it would take a few days for the injected medication to work and the pain to subside.

"I wanted to meet you, is all," Maddy said.

Dr. Carrington smiled and put out his hand. "How do you do, Maddy Moss. Welcome to my world."

"You are too handsome," she said, beaming at him. Maddy needed a doctor all to herself. That doctor was in the same practice as Dr. Dunn, the impatient dementia tester. Was he looking to declare incapacity in Maddy? I didn't feel it should be easy to call an elder incapacitated. I didn't feel this elder was incapacitated, even though something was wrong. I was vaguely nervous about Dr. Carrington. He didn't know Maddy. He didn't know me.

I had stayed away from the doctors on this island, saying to myself, "The island is your sanctuary. Keep your privacy and don't work as a guardian in this tiny town. Now you're in an island doctor's office with an elder. Did you think this out well enough?" I reminded myself, I did not want to do guardian work in my own back yard. Also, safety was an issue. There were several people in my life that I didn't want to know where I lived. My address was a secret.

I made Maddy another liverwurst sandwich with lettuce and tomato from my house. And then I went home for my supper. Later, I rode my bike to her house, just two blocks. Maddy was sleeping on the couch. I didn't disturb her.

The next morning, I was on my way to Saint Sandton to check on my wards when I got a call on my Bluetooth from Betty Picard. She was with Maddy.

"Oh yes," I said. "How do you do, Mrs. Picard?"

"Are you coming here today?"

"I could be there by 3:30 this afternoon."

I would include Betty? After all, she was sitting beside

Maddy right now? Maddy needed attention and Maddy wanted to choose for herself. I hoped this situation could be mended by inclusion.

Betty Picard discussed the idea of having someone stay with Maddy at night. I told her I knew sitter agencies. She said "Oh. Can't you do it?"

"No, I don't do home health or companion services." I answered.

I figured I had work to do. Maddy needed a softer bed, a chair that was comfortable, therapy for depression, and much better food, and maybe assisted living was in the future. I felt Maddy needed a few months of improvements on the status quo before anything could be decided upon.

I went to the Adult Protective Services meeting. This invitation only meeting took place once a month, where lawyers, guardians, social workers, and investigators discussed in confidence problems they might have with cases. Mary, my mentor guardian, had invited me to this "inner sanctum," and I felt accepted and welcomed because of her.

I checked on my wards and clients in Saint Sandton: Agnes, Sophie, Dorothy, and Shirley, a beautiful, elegant black woman who had had a stroke. There were no difficulties with any of my clients.

On my way back to the island in my trusty Prius, I bought free-range chicken, tomato basil soup, and whole grain bread at Whole Foods ($22.16). I dropped in to see Joy Kinkaid and arranged for a nighttime home health sitter for Maddy. When I arrived, Maddy was asleep on the couch. I put away the groceries in the kitchen and made a cup of tea for Maddy.

"How is the pain, Maddy?" I asked once she woke up.

"Better, thank you."

"Good."

Mrs. Picard arrived at 3:30 p.m. with Lidoderm patches prescribed by Dr. Carrington for Maddy's pain. I saw that Betty Picard was very put together, a beauty. Did I sense the arrogance Maddy had described?

Joy Kinkaid arrived to discuss a contract for night companions. Mrs. Picard said she was power of attorney for Maddy, so Joy needed her to sign the papers.

I hesitated. I thought, "No. Maddy can sign for herself."

Maddy hesitated, too, and then said, "Okay, Betty can sign."

When Joy left, I went over some things with Betty and Maddy. I felt Maddy needed a memory foam mattress pad on her bed and a reclining chair because she fell asleep in the uncomfortable chair in the living room.

"I can buy that, if—"

"No. I'll buy it," Betty said.

"Walmart has the best mattress topper," I said. "Three inches. It's about $250."

"Okay."

"Maddy, you need better nutrition," I said. "You seem malnourished to me."

"No. She. Is. Not!" Betty said. "She eats a good meal at the club every day."

Betty was defensive. Was Betty looking down her nose at me? I wanted to try to bring her and Maddy back together, if she would let go of the defensiveness. I hoped she actually wanted a better life for Maddy. For now, she seemed frustrated and impatient with her. Was she impatient with me too?

When Betty left, I prepared mashed potatoes, butternut squash, and chicken for Maddy. I gave her the evening pills. We sat in chairs and chatted.

Maddy said she was afraid Betty was angry with her for hiring me. I was sitting in Maddy's chair facing the door. She warned me about the chair. She was in that chair every night since she knew they were returning from two months in their summer home in Maine. Maddy told me she was vigilant, watching the door in case the Picards walked in. She had feelings of dread but hope too. "Maybe, they'll be my old friends again and come in and chat." Oh! Maddy *wanted* their friendship, so I would watch and learn.

The night sitter, Sally, arrived at 9:00 p.m. I went home at 9:30 p.m.

I called Sarah to give her an update about the day.

"Mrs. Picard was here this morning—"

"What was she doing there!"

"She called me." I said.

"Maddy asked that we keep the Picards away from her," Sarah insisted.

"Oh. I wasn't clear on that, I guess."

The next morning, very early at 6:15 a.m., I went by to check on Maddy and her sitter. The Picards were there!

"What is going on?" I asked cautiously.

Mr. Picard was silent. Mrs. Picard told me, "Maddy has been sitting totally still without talking for three hours. In the middle of the night, Maddy woke up and called 911."

Sally said she intercepted the call. Sally insisted she called me, but my phone said she didn't call me. I wished she had. So, Sally called the Picards at 3:00 a.m.

I asked Sally if she could make breakfast now. Betty wanted me to take Maddy to the hospital. When I asked why, the Picards left. I also went home to change my clothes. I checked on Maddy and Sally again. Maddy was asleep. Sally agreed she would stay until I returned.

I had a commitment at a bank at 8:15 a.m. to talk to the staff about guardianship and the newest, more-specific power of attorney laws. A new power of attorney now required the inclusion of the specific wishes of a person. It could no longer be a generalized two-page standard document that included generally all financial and health matters called "durable."

At the request of the bank manager, I talked with the whole staff before the bank opened to the public that day, about the idea that a guardian is a fiduciary, a person with whom it's safe to develop special trust, and that the law now stated a guardian could not receive a fee for holding power of attorney for someone. I held power of attorney for members of my family and friends. I was an executrix for three of them and I had held power of attorney for two of my clients in the past two years. And I did not request a fee for this responsibility to date. So cool. The court did not oversee a POA. I explained that there was safety on both sides of that agreement with the court as witness and I was most comfortable with my favorite way of being a guardian: voluntary guardianship. It was a safer form of power of attorney because both family guardians and professional guardians are vetted to be fiduciaries; it was good to have the court as a scrutinizer, with checks and balances. It was good protection for an elderly person who needed a little more help but could be clear about what they needed or wanted. The best thing about voluntary guardianship was that a person didn't lose their civil rights. The ward could petition to cancel the guardianship just like they could revoke or cancel a power of attorney at will.

I arrived back at Maddy's at 9:30 a.m. Mrs. Picard was present, and she reprimanded me for leaving. I explained to her that I had a meeting elsewhere, and Sally had agreed to be there until I returned. Mrs. Picard said she would now call the ambulance. I saw that Maddy was afraid.

"Why does an ambulance need to be called?" I asked. Mrs. Picard ignored me. A minute later, loud sirens sounded; three policeman and two big, rough-looking ambulance guys crowded the apartment. This was brutal! This was the difference between calling Westbrook Fire Station quietly and calling 911. It was overly dramatic. This was not my idea of a simple personal assistant job. This now had conflict in it ... and fear. It seemed to be designed to frighten Maddy? Really? Why?

Betty Picard told me to go with Maddy to the hospital, and I followed the ambulance in my car. Maddy was admitted immediately. I brought Maddy's medication list for the nurse to see dosages and Maddy's library book.

I called the neurologist I knew in Saint Sandton to see who she trusted in Westbrook to look at Maddy. Dr. Spain (a neurologist) examined Maddy. An MRI and scan tests of her lower body and legs were ordered. Maddy was again in a lot of pain, so the nurses brought a special kind of mattress. I stayed until 6:00 p.m. Maddy wanted me there to witness and listen with her. This was my normal routine when someone was in the hospital. It was advocacy.

I was quite weary. I thought, gosh, this was supposed to be a small job on the side to support my cash flow while I developed my guardianship/care management business. This was becoming a difficult crisis. I was unsettled about my role in it.

How should I be? I was confused about the Picards. I was confused about Maddy's fear. But her pain was real. I focused on that. Why was she in a hospital?

Oh dear. Did they want to have her declared incapacitated? Was that necessary? I tried not to feel pissed off. The sitter woke them up at 3:00 a.m., and now they were pissed off. Were they punishing Maddy as if she were a naughty child?

I was hoping Maddy could recover. She was hoping to recover!

The previous night, I had thought to find a way to include the Picards. Maddy was torn up about them. Was she attached? Co-dependent? She was definitely afraid of them. But why? They didn't listen, for sure. They talked about her, not with her. They didn't have to send an army of thugs to retrieve her and take her to the hospital because of her pain. Were they afraid of Maddy? Oh boy. I needed more wisdom. Perhaps I needed expert advice.

"Fear is dangerous. People are good."

– Brene Brown

Okay. That helped.

Since I was an outsider, new to their community, I was sure I was already suspected by the Picards by my very existence in Maddy's life. I got it, but I was beside Maddy now. After my experience with Violet, I knew I was the right person to stand beside Maddy and keep her out of the imprisonment all elders feared. However, any conflict was against my feeling that my own home had to be protected from my job, that the beach and waters around the island were sacred, my daily meditation.

I was slightly better known in the bigger, more-secure-in-themselves town to the south where my mentor guardian and others worked. But only a few people really knew me. Guardian work is confidential. Only a few ever know what any guardian really contributes. Only a few people knew for sure that I was a good person.

I knew myself. I had an innate sense of confidence in my advocacy and I believed my integrity showed. I knew everything showed on my face. I could not lie. Because I could never wipe the truth of how I felt off my face, luckily that honesty was coupled with an innate softness of heart. I trusted these qualities to shine through. I thought it was why Maddy was able to tell me her deeper truth.

But, here in Westbrook, I was out-and-out disliked by guardians June and Marianne. I was warned not to step on their toes. Would they not swoop in and take the route that Violet took? Could Maddy be taken into guardianship by them and their friends at Adult Protective Services?

I decided to work with a certified geriatric care manager and avoid guardianship in a town that was resistant to outsiders, especially guardians.

Maddy had begged Sarah to keep the Picards away from her. But Betty was in Maddy's apartment with her that very first Monday. How did she get there? It was confusing. I was confused. I was confused about my role. I called Sarah.

"Why are you so sure that the Picards should be kept away?" I asked.

"I think they want her money," Sarah answered.

"Do you have any proof of that?"

"They charge $300 more a month for that hovel of an apartment than anyone else around here pays."

"That's not enough."

"Betty Picard is a controlling bitch, and everyone around here is afraid of her!"

"You weren't clear about any of this last week," I said.

"I'm sorry. I guess Maddy must have called Betty Picard. She knows that number by heart."

And I thought this was going to be fun.

I wanted fun! Maddy was funny the day I met her. She was smart and perceptive and hopeful. That was before the Picards came back to town. Now Maddy was in distress. She felt panic in the middle of the night, but I didn't see incapacity. Maddy was still in agonizing pain.

The next morning, I asked a nurse about the scans. The nurse found the scans buried in yesterday's orders. Was that a mistake? I went back to Maddy's apartment to pick up the I-cap vitamins requested by the nurse, hearing aid batteries, and Maddy's bible.

When I returned to the hospital, Maddy begged me to keep "them" away from her. She said she couldn't appear vulnerable in front of them. I explained to Maddy that a power of attorney document doesn't have that kind of power. She could speak for herself. They had a responsibility to serve her wishes. She didn't believe me.

"Betty lost me," she said. "She treated me like a pony on a string."

I called Betty Picard.

"Why is Maddy so upset with you?" I asked.

Betty was impatient. "She is only mad at us," she said, "because we want her to go to assisted living and she doesn't want to." With this, Betty dismissed me and the subject.

Meanwhile, I saw my other clients and wards in Saint Sandton. Thank goodness everyone was in good shape. On my way back home, I joined Maddy in MRI holding. She had a bone scan and MRI of her lower region, back, and left hip.

Sarah arrived at 5:30 p.m. as Maddy was returned to her room. I was happy to go home.

Sarah phoned me later to say that she'd persuaded Maddy to go live at Serenity Cove assisted living.

The next morning, I started to form a care plan and budget for Maddy. I left the rough draft for Sarah on her front stoop. I wanted her additions and comments.

They had great food at Serenity Cove, so that would solve the nutrition problems. Maddy needed to choose the new apartment herself. They had a pool there, so she would need a personal trainer for the pool activity Sarah had started with Maddy over the previous two months. She would need transition support. Christmas was coming so she would need more social time at Christ Church, and with friends.

I created a rough care plan for Sarah to discuss with Maddy:

IN A FEW MONTHS: After Maddy feels more at home in her new digs, I recommend a visit to the Dementia Institute for a proper assessment of the degree of dementia or is it even dementia? The degree of duress and depression, including tests to rule out dementia, such as testing for vitamin deficiencies. Take into consideration that Maddy shows signs of psychological abuse and/or paranoia, real and/or imagined. Her fears might be based in reality. A visit to a specialist for bone–muscle improvement would be wise. I suspect this will improve on its own with proper nutrition.

GOAL: To improve quality of life. Support Maddy's own

willingness to thrive with action. Confidential budgeting and money management by an arm's-length fiduciary trust company would reassure that Maddy has an ally who includes her and reports to her directly around paying bills and the general state of her affairs. Maddy, by exercising her right to know her finances each week, will feel secure again. When Maddy is validated with better emotional support from me and others, I believe the friendship with the Picards, which Maddy does want, can be reaffirmed successfully.

## Hospital, Day 3, 8:30 a.m.

Neurologist Dr. Lu examined Maddy and felt the only problem was an inflamed bursa.

"We heard last night that there were bone chips floating," I said. He shook his head no.

I saw Dr. Carrington at the hospital and told him I believed in Maddy's right to self-determination. He nodded and walked away.

The Picards visited Maddy; I felt I could not honor her request to keep them away. When they tried to talk with her, Maddy began talking gibberish. In front of them, she looked crazy and self-sabotaging. It shocked me. I'd never seen her like this before. Finally, as they got up to leave, Betty Picard smiled warmly at me.

Any warmth at all was unexpected. Did I trust it?

"Bring us your bill this afternoon," she said. "Do you know where we live?"

"I think so." Was I seeing Betty Picard, really?

I wonder, had I gone to talk with Betty that afternoon, to take that smile as an opportunity, to see if I could make friends with her, to give her my CV and reference letters, I might have had a chance to become the hand-holder in the team. That would have been a better use of my time. Instead, between noon and 2:00 p.m., I tended to other business: bills and guardian administration for my wards. The next morning, I was leaving for a week away with my family up north. I had a lot to do.

Betty Picard phoned me to say I needn't stay with Maddy that afternoon.

"That's okay," I said. "I can visit with her." She did not like that. So, then I really wanted to stay with Maddy; I rushed over to the hospital as fast as I could.

When I got to the hospital, Maddy was not in her room. I found her in the MRI suite, again. She was all wrapped in a white blanket, head and all, only tiny bits of nose uncovered. It had been an MRI of her head for signs of dementia plaques.

She was delirious with fear. She was delirious from the way they moved her about. She told me they hurt her. Did they upset her on purpose? I sensed an evaluator was coming soon. I hoped my suspicion about disturbing elders to upset them and make them look nuts was wrong. This was the hospital that had called the guardians about Violet. I wondered about their elder care policies.

Back in her room, I spent an hour holding Maddy's hand, calming her, allowing her to vent her fear. I wanted her to do well, and by the time the doctor arrived, she was calm.

## 3:00 p.m.

The mental capacity evaluator arrived—Dr. McHatty. He was the one Maddy had refused to see two months ago. He was the psychologist Betty meant to use to condemn Maddy to a power of attorney she didn't want—or to save Maddy from herself, her "less than" self, her "ungrateful to Betty" self. This was a fast-moving train. Could I work something out for Maddy?

It turned out he was a great guy. By then Maddy had recovered from the harrowing MRI. She was charming with him. She told him she didn't want the Picards to be in control of her and, when she spoke of them, she started to go off, started to show … terror? And then the terror caused her to withdraw into bits of gibberish. I knew the doctor saw this.

I told him I believed with good food and her other needs met, and relief from excruciating pain, Maddy would feel more herself within a month. I asked if he would retest her in a month. He liked that idea and then asked me to leave the room. He had to test Maddy alone. She liked him well enough to agree to it, and I liked him too.

Dr. McHatty tested Maddy for twenty minutes and then came out of the room. He told me Maddy had a level-two dementia diagnosis (a very mild decline). He suggested we call Adult Protective Services. Really? I only feared more of the isolating strategies that go with exploitation. I wasn't sure. Oh dear.

The Picards were cold toward Maddy. Yes, they were understandably fed up after five years; however, Maddy should have what she wanted. She wanted the right to make her own decisions. If she needed supported decision making, okay then. She didn't need to be declared incapacitated to get some support.

Maddy had clearly told Dr. McHatty what she had told me: "I will not change my will, but please, Betty and Jerry, I do not trust you to help me with my well-being while I'm alive."

Dr. McHatty and I talked in the hallway about a second option: rather than calling Adult Protective Services, could we try a more diplomatic approach to the Picards? Perhaps, Dr. Carrington could do that for Maddy. The doctor said he was willing to suggest it to Dr. Carrington and ask for his help. I liked that idea.

I called Philippa, the geriatric care manager and advisor, and asked for advice. I told her Maddy seemed terrorized by the people holding her power of attorney, people she had known for twenty-five years. They did not like her. They seemed fed up. It must be uncomfortable for them because Maddy had turned against them. She talked gibberish only when they visited her;

she was completely normal when she talked with me or with her friend Sarah.

"I cannot put my finger on the truth of the matter," I said.

Then Philippa said, "Follow the money."

"Excuse me? What did you say?"

"Follow the money."

"But they're already rich."

She laughed at me.

I told Philippa that the psychologist in the hospital advised me to call Adult Protective Services. Since Philippa started at Adult Protective Services as an investigator, she told me to first threaten the Picards with calling Adult Protective Services unless they gave control back to Maddy.

Did I have the courage to threaten these people? I realized I was afraid of them too. Was it that Maddy was afraid and I was affected by that, or did I have real reason to be afraid? That told me, right then and there, that I should call Adult Protective Services to express my confusion.

It was the law that I had to have concrete evidence of abuse, neglect, or exploitation, or I could be penalized for false reporting. I wished they would accept confusion; there are penalties for unsubstantiated claims.

Did Adult Protective Services have animosity toward me?

They shared an office with June and Marianne who wanted me out of their way. Oh, boy. I didn't trust the place I needed to trust. They had plucked Violet from this very hospital and petitioned the court for guardianship with their friends, Marianne and June. I felt very uncomfortable.

I didn't want Maddy in that kind of guardianship, but I didn't want her treated badly by her friends either.

I couldn't say I suspected exploitation. Isolation is emotional abuse. I wracked my brain for concrete examples of abuse, neglect, and exploitation. I was feeling exhausted.

Then Sheila, nurse-sales person with Serenity Cove next door, arrived. She was curt. She told me to leave the room. She would not make eye contact with me. She met with Maddy for ten minutes, and Maddy refused to sign the admitting paper for Serenity Cove. I sensed fear as Sheila came out into the hallway.

I learned that Maddy had to sign herself into the rehab floor.

I asked Sheila, "But don't the Picards have power of attorney?"

"They do not have a complete power of attorney," she said.

Maddy was asking for a lawyer. Only the signature page of the Serenity Cove contract was presented to her to sign. It wasn't a proper document. Of course, she wouldn't sign it. Presenting one page insulted her.

"Where is the whole contract?" She was her sensible self.

I resolved to get her a lawyer who would actually represent her. She had told me her existing lawyer felt kind of "slimy" to her. I suspected he didn't work for her.

"The Picards are kicking Maddy out of her apartment," Sheila said.

That was mean! Mean landlord-type language.

Sheila's eyes bulged at me as she said, almost yelling, "The Picards are banking power of attorney for Maddy! They've already paid $35,000 for a month at the rehab at Serenity Cove."

"Gosh," I said, "Can't we get the doctor to turn the 'observation' word to 'treatment for severe pain'? That way, Medicare will pay for rehab, and Maddy can save that $35,000."

Sheila ignored this and asked if I knew any relatives, however distant, who could sign the paper. Then I got it. Sheila had a financial quota to meet. She had to get that paper signed! It was Friday night. The end of her quota month. She glared at me, in my face and desperate.

I was worried about the horrible day Maddy had endured. Sheila and I lost our tempers. I accused her of being aggressive toward Maddy.

She screamed, "You weren't in the room!"

That's right, but I watched through a crack in the door. I apologized, but Sheila snatched away the insulting signature-page from the Serenity Cove contract.

Then, I tried to help. I reassured Sheila that Sarah was Maddy's very good friend and in the morning, Sarah would help Maddy. "Please present the whole document." Maddy definitely needed a lawyer, but it was the end of business on a Friday night.

Sheila had told me too much. She didn't know she'd told me that the Picards were lying about their power of attorney. Maddy still had legal capacity to decide for herself!

## 6:00 p.m.

I felt exhausted. I went home to think things over. I called the Picards and apologized on their answering machine for losing my temper with Sheila. I called my friend, Sheila's sales director, Sheila's boss, to ask her to help me apologize for losing my temper with Sheila. My friend didn't return my call.

I didn't mean to lose my cool. I felt terrible; it was undignified. I realized, just as Sheila was pressured to meet her sales quota on a Friday night, I was also frustrated because any lawyer I trusted who could help Maddy was gone for the weekend. Why was a crisis always on a Friday, in the late afternoon, damn it! And I was leaving for the North in the morning.

## 7:00 p.m.

"Can you come over?" a nurse asked on the phone. "Maddy's asking for you."

I went back to the hospital; Maddy was dressed and wanted to leave. Sarah arrived at 8:30 p.m. Sarah told me that the Picards wanted to fire me.

"They said you are nothing but a forty-hour course. Serenity Cove hates you too."

"Really?" I asked. "You know what? You and Maddy hired me. You can be sure I have Maddy's best interest at heart. I'm not going anywhere."

The home health sitter arrived at 9:00 p.m. and I went home. I was in shock. This felt like a vicious situation. This was not good for Maddy. I considered staying, canceling the planes, canceling everything. I slept on it.

Saturday morning, Sarah escorted Maddy to Serenity Cove and stayed with her. This was best; Sarah was a good friend to Maddy. I was grateful. I could think things out in my sanctuary right here.

This kind of drama served Betty Picard. She was going to be the one to call the shots for Maddy. And she was in the process of having Maddy declared incompetent to handle her own affairs so that she could get a full, durable power of attorney.

For now, Jerry Picard had the weak power of attorney prepared years ago, smartly limiting and signed by Maddy and Harry. If Betty was not so controlling, she wouldn't need a stronger power of attorney. If Betty had been the least bit loving, if she had uttered one word of respect for Maddy, I would have been ecstatic with relief.

The Picards' power of attorney for the bank was still operating, obviously. They wrote a check for $35,000 to Serenity Cove on Maddy's behalf ... unnecessarily, because I felt she was eligible for Medicare. Dr. Carrington would only have had to sign for "treatment for pain" rather than "observation." Why didn't he do that?

I started, even more seriously, reporting events, trying to make sense of it all. Since Sarah was with Maddy, I stayed away for the weekend. I canceled my flights. I canceled my meetings. I apologized to my mother up north. She understood. I needed to research. This felt all wrong and I couldn't put my finger on it.

Could a person in fear of someone speak gibberish? I looked it up. Yes. People in terror could. I felt shaken by how Maddy was being disrespected; They said I was hated. They said Maddy was crazy. Was Maddy terrified for good reason? Yes. Could it be treated? Could she recover? Maddy wanted to heal and be happy?

On Monday morning, I called Dr. McHatty to see if there was a strategy to ask Dr. Carrington to gently suggest the Picards resign from Maddy's power of attorney. He said he could ask, but Dr. Carrington might not agree. Dr. McHatty said that on Sunday he checked on Maddy and met Sarah. He felt that Maddy was fine (she was perfect when she was with her friend, Sarah) and all was well.

I checked on Sarah. Sarah told me that Maddy was in a cavernous room at Serenity Cove and felt very frightened and that the Picards told Sarah to stop babying Maddy. They insisted on canceling the nighttime home health companions.

"Maddy must grow up," they said. "She doesn't have the money for that." However, an anonymous friend told Sarah that Maddy did have enough money, so were the Picards lying to protect Maddy's money—or their inheritance.

On Monday, I called lawyer Owen T. and we considered an emergency temporary guardianship (an ETG) or an ETG followed by a voluntary guardianship. Then I called Philippa.

"Can you go see Maddy and tell me what you think?"

Philippa met me at 4:00 p.m. and reported: "I saw two charming people, Maddy and Sarah, having a good time, and my conversation with Maddy was normal and pleasant."

Philippa let me know that an ETG was unnecessary. Maddy didn't seem to lack capacity. She told us she heard clearly that Maddy definitely did not want the Picards to be her power of attorney. Philippa also felt that a power of attorney or even a voluntary guardianship could be undone by the Picards by influencing or punishing Maddy.

I asked Owen to visit Maddy. He required a retainer.

I structured a strategy with him. I hoped that a voluntary guardianship would work, with Philippa's accounting company monitoring all checks and balances, with the court scrutinizing me. Sarah was adamantly against this idea.

"No guardianship!"

Maddy no longer had her checkbook. Sarah went to the apartment to discover that all of Maddy's files and checkbooks had been taken away. The Picards were protecting or controlling Maddy. There was no ability to retain Owen or alter the power of attorney as Maddy had requested.

Philippa was not as clarifying as I'd hoped; I wanted to advocate for Maddy's capacity. I felt Maddy was in jeopardy.

Then I got a call from Sarah saying that Maddy was out of it, refusing to eat, weak, and confused. I called Philippa again. By the time Philippa reached her, Maddy was again normal. But Philippa told me Maddy had 60/40 capacity. It could go either way.

The accountant, Mr. Cradle, visited Maddy at her request. Maddy trusted him, but he didn't give her any information. He didn't even need Sarah and the sitter to leave the room. It seemed that Maddy was already being treated as incapacitated. Did the Picards tell Mr. Cradle he wasn't required to give Maddy information? Did he think Maddy was being exploited?

Sarah and I thought Maddy was being grossly disrespected. Mr. Cradle suggested that creating a new power of attorney would cancel the old one. I knew this wasn't true. He did ask if Maddy would keep the Picards as co-signers on her bank account, and Maddy said she didn't want to.

Sarah helped Maddy write a letter to the Picards to say her truth—a suggestion from the accountant. He thought it wise to ask in writing for the Picards to step away from her business, to thank them, and request them to become her friends again.

After four days, I checked on Maddy. She had a wander-guard on her ankle, which would set off an alarm if she tried to leave. She was here against her will! It was a surprise and an outrage to me! I knew the receptionist well, from my eight months of hospice volunteer visits with Amelia.

"Is this necessary?" I asked. The receptionist gave me a dirty look.

Sarah didn't tell me about the wander-guard. Nor did Philippa. Why not?

"When can I get this off?" Maddy asked.

"Soon," I said.

Being in the film biz for a long time, I knew about getting things done yesterday and I had a work ethic to prove it. I got things done. Was I too fast to help this person? Or was I not fast enough? How could I get this prisoner-band-on-an-elder removed?

Maddy and I left the building with the receptionist watching and an alarm going off because of Maddy's wander-guard. The receptionist nodded saying, "It's okay. Go outside."

No wonder Maddy was stressed and frightened! She told me her pain level was tolerable and that she was constipated.

Sarah arrived with a letter. I read it to Maddy. Maddy added to it and agreed with it. Sarah read it aloud again and Maddy agreed.

I showed Maddy and Sarah up to the third-floor dining room for lunch. The food was excellent. Maddy ate well. She was walking well. Her pain was tolerable. She would be fine.

At lunch, I learned more about the accountant's visit from Sarah. That Maddy received zero information didn't seem right. Again, I wanted to call the adult protective services abuse line. Why was I afraid of them? Because I feared they'd helped my fellow Westbrook guardians to financially harvest Violet. Instead I again called my advisors.

Sarah took the letter away to make corrections and then brought it back for me to deliver. I didn't feel comfortable because she wanted me to deliver the letter alone.

I wanted to take my advisors advice. They said, "Get more formal protection. Maddy's letter is true and expresses her wish. Add a revoking document to it, signed by Maddy, who still holds capacity and, hopefully, will retain her right to self-determination."

I felt that this was a capacitated person with mild dementia, who was being terrorized. Maddy needed support, and healing, but she was already locked up with a wander-guard on her ankle, suggesting "You are a naughty child."

After Philippa read Sarah and Maddy's letter, she instructed me to score the doctor's paper saying Maddy had capacity. Sure, I wanted that too.

In the morning, I helped Maddy go to physical therapy. Sarah came to Serenity Cove, and Maddy signed her letter, a new letter to the accountant asking for the information she had originally requested, and one to Dr. Carrington requesting a letter of capacity. Sarah had been busy.

I expected to see the Picards, but they were nowhere to be seen and I had not spoken with them. I had no idea they had spies watching our every move with Maddy. I was busy getting Maddy a more comfortable mattress and having Maddy show the physical therapy staff that she could have a walker now and graduate out of the wheelchair. Success!

Lunch was a hot dog, and I let her know she could request food. I let the staff know she loved salads. They delivered a beautiful one.

Maddy requested some warm clothing and a clock. I took my neighbor, Jean, as witness and gathered clothing and her clocks. I took the clothes to her room at Serenity Cove and the sitter helped me put them away.

Then I drove around looking for the Adult Protect Services office; I still couldn't find it. Twentieth Street just didn't list the

Adult Protective Services anywhere. I ended up parked outside Owen's office.

An appointment with the doctor was scheduled for two days later. I called Philippa and asked, "Do you have a contract for bill payment we can add to our documents?"

She said, "If you had a power of attorney, I could make a contract."

Philippa was playing it safe. Did she sense problems? Could I trust her?

Owen drew a revoking of the power of attorney document for Maddy to sign. If she agreed, Owen would create a temporary document, giving me interim power of attorney until we could create a voluntary guardianship; It would offer both Maddy and me, protection, and assure transparency in the dealings with everyone around Maddy, yet Maddy would retain all her civil rights. This was the kind of guardianship I wanted for Maddy.

Owen came with me to Serenity Cove to meet Maddy for the first time, and we decided that if Maddy didn't want him to be her lawyer or didn't want to sign papers, we would cancel the plan. But it had taken two weeks to find a way for Owen to meet her.

We still needed the doctor to agree that Maddy had capacity, before the other papers would be valid. We also thought a voluntary guardianship could be drawn on November 3, two days in the future when Owen had some time.

Maddy was not in her room. I went looking for her.

Suddenly I saw everything in slow motion. The salesperson, Sheila, scowling at me. The policeman and the adult protection officer coming down the hall and entering Maddy's room. The policeman starting to rifle through my purse, which was sitting on the chair. I followed him into the room, asking, "What are you doing?"

The investigator from the adult protective services stepped forward and formally accused me and Sarah of exploitation and abuse. Sarah had asked that the nurse not give Maddy a pain pill before the accountant came to see her. Denying pain meds was abuse. Did the accountant set this situation in motion?

The policeman stepped into the hallway as Zena, the investigator from the adult protective services, asked Owen and me to join her in the boardroom across the hall.

I was still reeling from the accusation of exploitation. I was in shock.

"You're a guardian!" Zena said. "Why didn't you call us!"

I had no answer. I could not say "I wanted to but I don't like what you do to elders" This was not a good answer. There were many mixed messages. We were, rightfully, vacillating, hoping first and foremost that Maddy would recover well from her pain.

No one on my team working with Maddy wanted her to lose her rights. My team had wanted to try a less threatening way to approach the Picards, who were impatient with Maddy; they were definitely angry with her. Yet here they were accusing me and Sarah of exploitation. Who wanted us out of the way?

Whether or not the Picards were exploiting her, Maddy didn't want them handling her affairs; she wanted them as friends, she allowed them in turn to remain as heirs to her estate. They had been helping her for five years. Now she wanted a different situation for herself.

Why can't people hear elders say, "I don't want this"?

I thought her care plan should be more in-depth and had started creating a deeper care plan. I knew I was doing the right thing. I felt I was not alone. I had a team around Maddy advising me. I was serving Maddy and Sarah. We were all trying to avoid the declaration of incapacity. But here we were. I was acting without the court behind me. I had no authority. This was the "grey time" and things had just gotten really messy. Maddy was at the hospital, and now at the rehab next door, June and Marianne's colleagues from adult protective services have been called in to accuse me of exploitation. Gulp.

Now, Maddy was about to lose all control over her life? I wanted to fight.

"Maddy doesn't know you," Zena said to me. "She doesn't know Sarah. Doesn't know where she is or that she was in hospital last week. Maddy adores her best friend, Betty Picard."

Really? Maddy told Zena she doesn't know me? Had I been hearing Maddy correctly? Owen and I were sitting in the boardroom with Zena; we registered Maddy's testimony. We spoke to Zena as much as to each other. "Well then, our next step would be to create a guardianship." I didn't say much else. I was in shock.

Owen and I answered questions, but I don't remember what I said. Owen mentioned the hear-say that led our team to suspect Betty and Jerry Picard of exploiting Maddy. Later, Sarah said she told Zena a similar suspicion. Owen told me he'd recognized the Picards' strategy of isolating Maddy from anyone who could help her and believed it would be seen that way by the Adult Protective Services once they investigated fully.

The policeman stayed in the hall of Serenity Cove; he was an ominous presence. I heard him mutter, as I passed, "This is a civil matter. What am I doing here?" I was grateful for his message. I was also clearly aware of the animosity of Nurse Sheila, who was glaring at me from the lobby twenty feet away.

I was guilty of having thought I had enough resources around Maddy to figure out a way it could peacefully work out for everybody. Ridiculous. It could never work out. She was doomed. But I couldn't give up on her.

When Zena read the charge of exploitation, I wondered if the accountant had told the Picards that Maddy was taking concrete steps to remove them, to revoke the power of attorney. They had controlled everything and everyone in this scenario, including the doctors, their lawyers, and the police.

I was later reassured by those who knew me, "Don't worry.

Adult Protective Services will route out the truth of the matter. You will hear from them." I could never exploit an elder. I was glad to know people recognized me. I suspected June and Marianne, good friends with Serenity Cove, had something to do with this. Did they wish to steal Maddy?

I stayed with Maddy for a while that horrible day, but I couldn't stay so I asked home health if Maddy could have a sitter for two hours. I checked with Serenity Cove about an appointment with Dr. Carrington and they didn't have it in their books.

What kind of racket was this? I thought about Violet. Emergency room, then admitted to the hospital, then across the street to the rehab, and then some kind of imprisoning care ordered up for a feisty, mistrusting, wealthy widow who was a pain in the ass. She was naughty, behaving badly, and thus needing to be "kept safe," a euphemism for "restrained," "isolated," from people like us; pushed away, suspected of stealing, when we were really looking to manage things more transparently and in favor of protecting her right to self-determination with the doable support she needed at home. An aura of fear and shame was sprayed around like a soul-numbing perfume, inhibiting real friends from coming near, isolating Violet, isolating Maddy.

I went to see Colin, the owner of the assisted living facility for the mentally ill. He was an effective advocate. He was wise, and I was very confused. He felt my experience of being accused was weird. The idea that I was attacked like that seemed wrong, somehow, when I described a widow with slight dementia.

"Did she have money?" he asked.

"Yes."

Colin nodded. "Look at Howard Hughes or Leona Helmsley. They were imprisoned because they had money. Sure, they were made to look crazy and their behavior looked that way, but why? Because they couldn't trust anyone. They really couldn't! They were not advocated for. They were not helped out of crisis, because it was convenient and lucrative for those around them to have them worsen."

Isolation is so very dangerous for people who are vulnerable and in need of the right kind of protection.

People didn't ask why these famous, seemingly crazy people were acting as they did. They weren't listening. My mentor guardian, Mary was now saying to me, "Just keep doing your work. Show them how good you are. But don't speak! Don't speak." Mary said, "If you speak out and ask us to help this lady, we'll say 'no' because you will put us in jeopardy too. And don't involve Abby in this."

Did Mary think I was guilty of something? No. I wasn't going to join the secret guardian club. The sin was I complained to her about the conduct of a fellow guardian. The club was doing good for some people but for others, it was on an ethically shaky skinny branch, and Mary knew I refused to protect that club.

Mary's point: Annie, you might force us to reveal that we have sweetheart deals with the other guardians and their lawyers, who plotted to destroy you once you found fault with them and their practice of keeping an elder in a nursing home against her wishes. Don't all wards wish to go free, back into their former life, under their own control? That's why guardians are given authority to control people for their own good.

Once an elderly ward realized that they could do better with some help, they were open to collaboration. Could guardianship be a gentle calling, please?

## David and Goliath

Unfortunately, Dr. Carrington, our hoped-for advocate, was not in the loop and did not have privileges at Serenity Cove. But I was determined to honor Maddy's request for a declaration of capacity. I checked on Maddy and checked with Dr. Carrington's office and Serenity Cove. The appointment *was* scheduled, but there were no car arrangements with Serenity Cove, so I felt forced to cancel it. Then a nurse came to tell me I was authorized by Jerry Picard to drive Maddy myself. So, I did. We were five minutes late. Maddy was slow in navigating with her walker.

The Picards were there. Betty, trembling with anger, told me I could leave now.

Maddy sat far from them and told me to get over there with her, "Don't talk to them, and get me some water."

When Jerry Picard approached her, Maddy threw her water at him and hit him with her walker three times! She was escorted away, into the doctor's office, and Betty Picard jeered at me, "We will drive her back. You can go." I gave my card to the receptionist and said if Maddy didn't want to go with them, to call me or Serenity Cove. Then, I tried to reason with the Picards.

"Surely we all want the best for Maddy," I said.

"You just tried to kidnap Maddy!" Betty accused, acting fearful. Really? Did they not just authorize me to drive Maddy there a half an hour earlier? It felt like a grand performance in the doctor's office, of animosity and accusation against me.

I went out to the car, shaking hard. I phoned Philippa. She told me to go back in and appeal to the Picards for collaboration and communication. I couldn't believe that anyone who worked with me, for Maddy's wellbeing, thought I didn't respect her. Couldn't we all please just root for Maddy to recover and have her wishes heard?

## In the doctor's waiting room

I went back in, still shaking some, still afraid of them. I told the Picards I was a professional and that I had Maddy's best interest at heart, and I was sure they did too. I asked that we talk it out in peace.

I told them they couldn't dismiss me because it was unwise to keep Maddy's friends and her assistant from serving Maddy. I asked them to make peace with me and I started asking questions about what was going on.

Dr. Carrington came out from his time with Maddy and told all three of us that he thought he understood what was happening and wanted to see us in his office. He had a few patients to see first.

Maddy was whisked out of the office in a wheelchair and taken back to Serenity Cove by limo. The Picards and I waited … in silence.

When we were escorted into Dr. Carrington's office, Betty said I was poisoning Maddy against them.

"No way," I said. "I'm trying to find a way to have peace between you and Maddy. Maddy wants you away from her business and her health matters, hoping against hope that you can be friends. She desperately wants friendship with you. She's grateful to you, but she doesn't want to be controlled. Very few vulnerable people need to be controlled."

"Maddy can't afford home health companions," the Picards said. "And why are you ordering them?"

I explained to the Picards that the day before I had called home health to say I had to leave Maddy to go to my other clients. Maddy had just been through an interview with a policeman and adult protective services. Uniforms meant trouble was brewing. She was afraid. I was concerned. Home health sent someone for only two hours. I reminded Betty Picard that she was the one who initially requested home health, and Maddy had appreciated it.

It became clear that, although they didn't visit Maddy at

Serenity Cove, Serenity Cove was phoning them with every move made with Maddy.

I felt that Maddy's words, "Betty lost me. She treated me like a pony on a string," were true. Betty had everyone on a string; I feared she had me on a string too. I felt I was going to be hung out to dry and no one would give a damn. That must be how Maddy felt. I studied Betty's silent husband.

The doctor sat down with us, and Betty continued.

"You are nothing but a forty-hour course," she said, demeaning me in front of the doctor. I felt her influence at work, diminishing and excommunicating the two advocates who'd had the courage to stand up for Maddy.

Betty was surprised to hear I had other clients and wards. I told her this was supposed to be a ten- to twelve-hour per week personal assistant job for a robust elder two blocks from my house. All my other clients were in Saint Sandton.

Dr. Carrington said the stress had caused Maddy to withdraw into dementia and now paranoia. The doctor was very diplomatic and told me to be careful what papers I had Maddy sign. I nodded. He essentially stopped Maddy's right to sign for herself because, right then and there, he declared her to lack capacity, ending her right to present her letter to the Picards.

"Maybe out of this, something good will come, after all," he said.

He recommended guardianship, which suggested to me he knew Maddy was overcontrolled by Betty Picard. He thanked me, saying I could reduce the animosity felt if I stepped away. I nodded. He suggested David as guardian.

Then, Betty Picard gloated. "Does that mean I have the say, now?"

"For the moment," Dr. Carrington said.

"We could have avoided all this," Betty said, "if that assessment appointment with Dr. McHatty wasn't canceled two months ago."

The doctor said that stress was the cause of Maddy withdrawing so far. I was sad about the stress too. The doctor said he definitely heard from Maddy that she didn't like Serenity Cove and suggested Summer Place assisted living facility.

"Maddy is essentially healthy and could live ten years more."

Betty Picard gasped audibly. Was this not in line with her plans? On the way out, she told me to send my invoice to her and we parted ways.

I would not send any invoice to the Picards. There was too much conflict. If there was to be a guardianship, I would be part of the team that looked into Maddy's situation and, perhaps, I would invoice then. It could go through the court for approval through the guardian—I intended to select that guardian.

Shortly afterwards, I sent Dr. Carrington information with a list of other guardians and guardianship lawyers. I suggested Kaye Kendrick as guardian. I also sent a care plan to the Picards, with resources for them and Maddy regarding the healing of their friendship.

That same day, Sarah was brutally questioned by Zena, the adult protective investigator, for an hour and a half. After that Sarah went to Maddy and said, "Maddy, I understand you withdrew and told the policeman, you adored Betty Picard. You also said you didn't know me or Ann. You knew us very well!" Sarah told her she couldn't be there for her anymore. Then, Sarah walked out of Maddy's life.

Sarah called me with this information and also told me that Zena was out to get me.

I wrote to Sarah, saying that Maddy couldn't help but withdraw, being questioned by a policeman. That was too scary. Of course, she was going to go inside her shell. I knew that Maddy was now without the two people brave enough to stand up with her and let her be heard.

That evening, Maddy phoned me. "Where are you?" she asked me. "You are my mentor."

Oh, how I wanted to continue as her mentor! But I had to tell her I wouldn't be seeing her for a while.

Maddy's night companions lasted a few more days and then they were canceled.

I met with Owen T. to petition for guardianship. He felt I would be a fine guardian for Maddy and wrote up papers.

I met with Sarah and asked if she would be the petitioner. She asked if the Picards would see her name on the paper; I said yes.

Sarah was afraid to petition. She was afraid that she would lose her job as assistant to the town clerk. Mrs. Picard's son, the policeman, saw her every day at city hall. The Picards could use their influence to get her fired and she wanted to keep her job.

I therefore stepped away as Dr. Carrington suggested. Instead I worked hard to persuade colleagues I trusted to replace me.

Ten days later, I checked on Maddy at 7:30 a.m. We were happy to see each other. She showed me Sarah's telephone number hidden between two pairs of underpants and pointed to a rainbow sticker saying that was all she had left of me. There was no telephone. I told her strongly that she must eat and exercise, and she agreed to it. I gave her a photo of a rainbow. I asked her if she had a good visit with her friend from Vermont and she shrugged. I hugged her.

I attended Local Care Conference the same day in Westbrook and learned that two declarations of incapacity will do for a power of attorney to take over an incapacitated family member's or friend's affairs. I had thought they needed three as guardians did… They already had their two for Maddy. Damn.

November 9th court records showed that Betty Picard,

alone, became power of attorney of an incapacitated person with the initials MM.

I attended the Adult Protective Services brainstorming meeting, hoping to give voice to my promise to Maddy that she would be heard. I wanted to tell Maddy's story, but I didn't speak about the case. I was hesitant and then my opportunity evaporated. My fellow guardians had told me Zena would call me again. My colleagues said, "Don't beat yourself up. Stay silent. Trust that they will investigate. They'll figure out the truth. Do not worry."

It was a warlike situation about control. The team that worked on this case together, including Sarah, Ann, Philippa, and Owen, always had Maddy's wishes and happiness and ultimately her protection in mind. There was no intent whatsoever to exploit Maddy M. There was respect. I was sure about it. Well maybe Philippa had chosen discretion somehow, because now she was not returning my calls.

Right. I was clearly very bad at saving my own ass.

Indeed, we witnessed Maddy fighting for her life and battling with herself too.

The old golfer buddies drew their swords at us, Maddy's new friends, as soon as there was a whisper of a suggestion that we could help them with a difficult transition and hopefully end with friendship. Nope. They drew their swords. Our team moved to protect and thwart the ambition for control that caused them to attack more brutally. Maddy, it seemed, was not ever going to be heard or considered.

Could my trying to make friends with Betty Picard have been a success? No. I believed more and more that her goal was to isolate Maddy and secure for her children Maddy's inheritance. She had earned it for five long years and her goal now was to punish Maddy for making so much trouble.

I vacillated between hope and terror for Maddy. I wanted to stand for her and her wish to be heard. I decided to speak out at the next Adult Protective Services team meeting.

## Maddy Moss
## Honoring her truth

*Partly read to the Adult Protective Services team members*

Recently I worked with a capacitated elder who wanted to ask her deceased husband's golfing buddies of twenty-five years to step away as her power of attorney. She wanted their friendship. However, she did not trust that they would help her care for herself or listen to her wishes, now that she was becoming more vulnerable with mild dementia. These friends seemed tired of her. Impatient with her. She saw that they wanted to take control of her life. This retired human-resources manager told me that this couple talked about her instead of with her, which she corrected by saying "I am here. Talk to me."

"Did they mean well? Maybe. Maybe not. Her desire was to ask them to stay friends with her, that if they stepped away as power of attorney, she would not change her will, meaning they would still inherit her estate. For that, please allow others who had been collaborating with her in their absence for two months to continue to collaborate with her about her transition to assisted living, her budgets, and future security while alive. She trusted that her advocates (me or others of her choice) would collaborate toward her true quality of life.

She was very afraid, actually in terror about what their reaction to her wishes would be. This was the reaction: They placed her in a facility she didn't want and placed a wander-guard on her ankle. Because she was there against her will, she became more frightened of them, and that stress caused her to further withdraw intermittently into confusion. She asked us to please keep them from visiting her.

With the help of the facility, which stood to gain financially by collaborating with these influential and influencing golfer buddies, they, as power of attorney, prevailed in controlling this elder and teaching the facility how to treat her: "For her own good."

She was a naughty child, wasn't she?

"When the advocates tried to help her communicate with the power of attorney in the form of a letter she dictated, she was further isolated. The two advocates for this elder (Ann and Sarah) and their expert advisors were brutally dismissed. How? The police were called by the golfer buddies. Zena, the adult protective services investigator, and a policeman interviewed Maddy, and she was so scared she denied knowing Sarah and Ann. Maddy told the policeman she adored Betty Picard. Zena told us Maddy did not remember that she was in the hospital last week and she did not know where she was now. The two advocates were promptly accused of exploitation. Not true. This was a lie.

The doctor then declared Maddy incapacitated, giving these golfer buddy friends full control of her life. Her phone was removed. Her golfer buddies declared that her advocates were the enemy and Maddy was to be protected from them. Sarah and Ann, now declared the enemy, were restrained from visiting Maddy.

Maddy's letter was never delivered, since her signature was now declared illegal. She was silenced. She was not treated like the dignified elder she truly was. Even if she had intermittent (terror) dementia or mild dementia, she had a will to live and she had a voice. She wanted to hope that she could recover. With the right kind of support, Maddy would have recovered.

With group therapy and kindness, and by listening, this situation could have been healed and the old friendship recovered.

To date, it is unknown whether these golfer buddies have acted on my recommendations about therapy, the newly suggested independent professionals, and the arm's-length financial advisors. The goal was to heal the lack of safety this elder felt. Please respect the real terror caused to this elder by this unnecessarily escalating imprisonment. Heartbreaking.

Sincerely, Annie B. Wagner NCG

## December 20, 8:30 a.m.

The Adult Protective Services meeting was full of lawyers and guardians and administrators. Christmas cookies were abundant. I was nervous because it had been almost two months since they accused me and Sarah of exploitation, and they had not spoken with me about it nor had I received a letter stating I had been exonerated.

I put up my hand. "I want to speak for Maddy M. who has not been heard," I said.

I read the first two paragraphs of the letter to them. I started to explain that Maddy no longer wanted to be dictated to by her friends. I explained that she seemed terrorized. When speaking with my team, she was clear, witty, and sane, and showed very few signs of dementia. A psychologist declared her to have only very mild impairment.

When she was with the golfer buddies, she spoke gibberish and self-sabotaged. She looked bad, crazy even, but I felt she could recover. She was being humiliated and felt terrorized.

"And I know this," I said, "because I felt terrorized myself by these influential-in-my-community, golfer buddies. I believe it is emotional abuse and I seek advice."

A nurse at the meeting asked, "Did you call Adult Protective Services?"

"Before I could, I was the one accused."

"MM is safe," the co-director interrupted. He was sitting directly behind me. I was relieved she was safe. (How was she "safe"?) "The case has been closed, with two persons suspected of exploitation. We have passed the investigation to the attorney general's office."

I was dumbfounded. They actually thought I was capable of exploitation.

Mary, my mentor guardian, sat at the other end of the table. She surreptitiously shook her head "no." Her eyes told me to shut up. Once we were outside the building, she told me, "You don't realize how powerful the people in that room are. You don't realize what they can do to you."

I was in legal jeopardy. This was intolerable. I didn't feel I could withstand this reality. That day, I phoned Owen T. My friend Abby, the parish nurse came with me when I met with him later that day. Owen gave me the number of a criminal lawyer. He explained that, if the police knock on my door, I must go with them, but I must not speak. As hard as that will be. I must tell them nothing. I must memorize over and over again: "I have nothing to say without the presence of my lawyer."

# The Delirium of Fear

There'll be a knock on my door? And something dreadful will happen to me? I'll be taken away to prison without a hearing? Justice will fail me!

How could I be guilty? Of what? Of staying in their game too long? Of trying to save someone from imprisonment? Of being told not to speak and not being able to shut up? I wasn't wise.

"Help her," I said, "Help her. She's being terrorized by those people! She's terrified."

I committed professional suicide. Speaking, speaking out, speaking too late, speaking badly ... speaking.

Now.

I am guilty of silence.

I am shunned on my sanctuary island. Despising stares appear on faces if they even bother to lift to my face. I can't speak. I want to run away. This feeling, please stop waking me in the night, all night. What is it! What have I done wrong? I am too emotional? I care. I care too much? Others know how to protect themselves. I don't know how. I don't know how. Ghosted. Held up as example. "See. Guardians are bad!" "I am good! I am good! I am good!"

"Just go away," they say.

I *do* look suspect! Because I *am* guilty. I failed an elder. When I speak for her or me, I sound guilty, weak, strange, out-of-body, and destroyed inside. I failed an elder in my care. I can't bear it. I am guilty. Come on, come, knock on my door. I am inside. I am inside the delirium of fear.

# CHAPTER SEVEN

# Christmas In A Locked Ward

"Hello, Ann." It was Sarah. "I visited with Maddy on Christmas Day. She's housed in the dementia unit at Serenity Cove. It's a locked unit. She's tied to a wheelchair. Shaking hands. Nurses tell me that Maddy keeps falling and banging her head on the floor. She has been in the hospital twice."

"Twice since I saw her in November?" I asked. "There was no invitation to join the Picard family for Christmas?"

"No," Sarah said. "Maddy told me, 'Tell Ann not to visit. It's too painful for me.' Maddy also said people could hurt you. She told me not to visit her anymore either."

Sarah asked if I wanted to meet and talk. I was too afraid and too betrayed. I said No. We said goodbye.

No one in my profession helped Maddy. No one! I had begged so many colleagues to help her.

Dr. Carrington. Was he involved or not? Advocating for her or not? Maddy told him, she didn't want to go to Serenity Cove. But now, she's locked up at Serenity Cove. That place is empty advertising. She's being restrained. If I talk, if I "interfere," they will arrest me.

There were no additional services for healing the fear and terror, allowing stress to claim this elder who was wanting to thrive when I met her.

Court Records told me: All by herself, Betty Picard was the only person named. She controlled Maddy Moss in every way.

Jerry abdicated, and Harry cried down from Heaven.

Maddy started bashing her head on the floor as hard as she could so they locked her out of her room. She bashed her head on any sharp thing she could reach. She wanted to hurry up and get it over with. She had no hope. It took two years for Maddy to finally leave her "safe" place.

## Maddy knew her fate. That is why she cried out for help and nobody helped her.

I sensed all along that this punishing course would be a death sentence for Maddy. That's why I could not bear to be stopped. Maddy did not commit suicide. Step by step, she was stressed and pushed to a shorter life. I couldn't stop it because I couldn't put my finger on it. I couldn't believe it. I was not experienced or jaded enough, not fast enough to stop it before I was disabled by the system of powerful lawyers that attacked me.

I still kept desperately trying to help Maddy, only sensing, not understanding the real truth of the matter. I recommended Kay Kline as guardian. And what happened to the comprehensive care plan I delivered to the Picards and the doctor in November?

The friends around me kept trying to tell me that I did everything I could; I went out on a limb. I was brutally stopped, and I still kept on trying. How could I jeopardize my own safety to that degree? I guess I hoped for support for Maddy from my colleagues.

I reached out all over the place. Help never came. No one helped her. The powerful lawyers at the top of the system chose to shut me up. The influential woman stayed influential. She could pay those high-priced lawyers. They delivered.

Can we see that intentionally stressing an elder will demoralize and destroy hope? Maddy saw it. Hence her cry for help, her terror.

I could not go free. I failed Maddy. I was haunted by that feeling for years. Finally I realized it was clear to all that I was a good person. It didn't matter. I was not a person at all to them. I was only an obstacle in the way of their plan. When I realized that, I was free to accept my responsibility in Maddy's demise. I was not experienced enough at that time.

I reached out to my own lawyer up north, a quiet Buddhist lawyer who knew me well. She was wise, and she believed, as I did, that all people are good at heart.

"The only mistake you made," Francis said, "was to too fervently advocate for one person in a multi-person situation. A hired gun will be shot down. You did not yet have wisdom about a particular thing. Now, from experience, you have more.

I was a hired gun? Really? Is that what I was? Is that what Maddy wanted?

Francis continued, "No man or woman is an island; there are co-dependencies everywhere, some healthy, some sick. Each person sees things from their own, sometimes warped, perspective, but if you are to work with a group, you have to see things from many perspectives and get good at that. There are many truths, not just one truth. Practice brings wisdom.

"Usually there are no 'baddies'—only people who have different motivations. Selfishness is the primary motivation of everyone, and it's not bad. It's safe to know and respect people for their motivations. You need to know the selfish motivations of the people in a group in order to work with them. It's good to know humans as the emotional beings they are, to expect their selfishness, and to love them for it. Compassion for all, not just those you think are deserving. Acceptance of the above is all you need to do what you want. This we can discuss so that you can make it your practice."

Yes, I was too fervent perhaps. I can't stand greed. I knew I was naive. I couldn't face that murder was taking place in this civil society. Maddy knew it. She kept telling us too.

Yes. Compassion for all…

"But it's not fair!" I said. "Where is the justice for Maddy?"

My friend, the retired judge, scolded me. "Are you so naive that you think justice has anything at all to do with the law? You cannot fall apart like this! If I fell apart every time a monster buggered an infant and we could not get justice in my courtroom, I could not do my job!"

And she was right. I had fallen apart. I could not do my job.

## Brave Face

I sent a letter to each lawyer with whom I had guardianship clients and told them I was innocent of any wrongdoing and that, ethically, I did nothing wrong. I also sent reference letters. There was silence.

After the Adult Protective Meeting told everyone in the room I was accused of exploitation, the guardianship lawyers I worked with definitely wanted to kick me off their cases.

Abby, the parish nurse and I continued to watch over Agnes, even though lawyer Amy P. declared the guardianship to be 'no longer needed" We collaborated with the "good" daughters. We tried to heal the daughter who lived in the discomfort of being accused of exploitation. Now, I felt her pain. She lived in the no man's land of accusation and only accusation, with little chance to redeem herself.

Abby sat with me many a time when all I could do was cry. I told her all the strength had gone out of me. She prayed a lot. She tried to remind me that I was a wonderful person and that these situations, while they seem so unfair and cruel, happened to many people she knew and that it would heal.

I told Noah K., Sophie's guardianship lawyer, that I wanted to resign. He said I had to replace myself as Sophie's guardian. I did. It took a long time, almost a year of putting on a brave face, while continuing to be Sophie's guardian.

"How did you get Marilyn K. to take the case?" he asked, impressed.

"Because I want the best for Sophie," I said. He shook my hand.

No lawyer but Owen T. lifted a finger to support who I was and what I had done for my clients.

"You are a little too emotional," he said, "but I would far rather work with you than the others."

When I said "hi" to Mary, my former mentor guardian,

basically cornering her in the parking lot of the Oaks Assisted Living, she told me, "You are okay for easy guardianships like Agnes, but you are not tough. You can't do this really."

Yes, I disappointed her. Yes, I am not tough today.

Recently, my neighbor came with me to clean out a house of one of Mary's wards. Professional guardians are taught to never go into a vacant house alone. Have a witness. So, Jim, my retired-chef neighbor, accompanied me. He was looking for charity work, and this certainly qualified. Jim freaked out when he saw what I did. He saw the trash, the filth, the fact that the house was disputed.

"This is dangerous!" he said.

Mary paid me $20 an hour to help her with her wards, and she was supportive really. But she didn't agree with me. I was not her kind of guardian. When I told her, "My heart was not into watching over her ward, Shirley" (because I was always holding back tears), she told our whole community, "Ann's heart is not into being a guardian anymore." I didn't mean that. I wanted to hold onto my certifications. I wanted to recover, not quit!

I retain my certifications and clearances today. My friend, the honorable Laura C., told me a year later, I was never going to be sent to jail, and indeed, no policeman has ever knocked on my door. Laura said it was bullies silencing me from a few powerful directions.

I was a great guardian for Isabella C. I tried everything I

could to spark her will to live. I did not fail her. It failed. I handed her over to Jackie, a tough old guardian who understood how to maintain a ward. I was not interested in simply maintaining a ward. If there was no engagement, no trying, I was truly not interested. Jackie said I spoiled Isabella. (Nah) Charlotte, the MSW got what I was trying to do with Isa, how hard I worked to recover her.

It was disappointing for Charlotte that I became a reputation nightmare. She mentored me in order to have a humanist guardian at the ready for her clients and I enjoyed the collaboration. But she couldn't work with me after she saw how hard-hit I was from the threats and character assassination. Guardians are supposed to have a thicker skin.

Charlotte knew the influential family that had accused me of exploitation. She was not going to stay on the wrong side of Westbrook's most important family. Her whole client base was in Westbrook. The same with the doctor, the prestigious nursing home with the high-pressure monthly quota for their nurse/sales people, the territorial guardians who were pleased to put a snake on my back. I heard that Mrs. Picard told her entire network to be afraid of me.

"Are you a fighter or a lover?" Colin had asked.

I guessed I was not a fighter.

I was nothing right then.

I persuaded Marilyn K. to take Sophie. Marilyn was a guardian and geriatric care manager who really felt humane to me. I told her it was not Sophie; it was me. So, she took Sophie and carried on my collaboration with her. I did everything I could to set Sophie up so that Marilyn didn't have a lot of work to do. I got Sophie's uncle to chip in a monthly allowance. I got a Medicaid-sponsored cell phone for her, since I wouldn't be paying her virgin mobile. I secured her chances with Compeer, the volunteer friendship program for the mentally ill. I did the required yearly financial and personal reports. I took Sophie to her doctor and received his yearly report, then prepared my final reports for the court.

I rented a storage unit. I stored all Sophie's valuable papers for three years. I photocopied them for Marilyn, as required. I told Sophie that my family was in crisis up north and I had to give up all my clients. Sophie forgave me, accepted Marilyn, and rewarded me by writing a poem:

To Ann,

Maker of memories to sweeten the bitter,
Chase away clouds of doubt and confusion.
Harbinger of possibility, hope for tomorrow.
You are and have given me all of this, Ann.
May God speed you to your family at this time.
Thank you for all that you have done,
Love, Sophie

PS. I saw two operas w/ Emily. Last night was great. Thanks again.

Fondly, Sophie

# CHAPTER EIGHT

# Holding Hands: A Good Death

**A year later**

It was mid-December. My stepfather couldn't breathe. He was very distressed, and so my mum and their live-in caregiver, Nicole, decided to call an ambulance. Ken and his son, Tony were placed in a small room in the ER for hours. The doctor could not or would not act to relieve Ken's suffering. Why not Halifax, Nova Scotia?

"Mr. East," the doctor said, "there's nothing we can do for you."

What was and wasn't happening to my loved ones? It was cruel. I called my hospice volunteer coordinator in Saint Sandton and asked what they would give medically to relieve Ken's panic at not being able to breathe. He had heart failure. He had dementia. She referred me to a hospice nurse.

"Morphine will greatly help him to breathe easier," a nurse said. She also gave me other palliative care formulas to request in the ER.

Tony didn't want to bother the busy doctors. I coached

him by phone, to ask for palliative care. The doctors said they had no bed for Ken. I coached Tony again. "We do not want a bed. We want a prescription and hospice at home." Ken would then panic again, and again because he could not breathe. Mum would call the ambulance. This went on for three more trips to two different Emergency Rooms. They simply sent Ken home with no support each time. Even with my coaching, Tony couldn't get the doctors to act.

So, I got on an airplane.

I hired a night nurse so mum and Nicole could get some sleep. I visited both emergency rooms, insisting that they help Ken. I called the government care coordinator in charge of my parents. She sent in public health nurses to lend support, and I continued to call the ER doctors. It seemed they could care less. The nurse standing beside me in mum's living room took the phone in support. The doctor was nonchalant as he said to the nurse, "She's really upset, isn't she?"

Finally, after two days of being constantly in their faces with demands, on Christmas day, a hospice doctor came out of nowhere and personally delivered the prescriptions to a pharmacy open on Christmas day. She was my hero.

We were in business. We formed a home health team schedule to provide Ken a good death. We recovered my mother from many days of stress and lack of sleep. The hired nurse and I stayed up at night with Ken. We had some pretty entertaining talks, and Ken felt no panic. He told us he couldn't decide whether to come back again as a redheaded woman or as a white horse.

He was half on earth and half moving to spirit, and he didn't seem to have dementia anymore. We were all living in the moment; he knew he was dying. Tony spent one of the last four nights with his father and had a similar feeling: great talks and no dementia. The last night, Ken got really raucous and struggled to get out of bed. We failed to keep him there as he slid to the floor. The ambulance drivers seemed to be there in a split second. They lifted Ken back into bed and arranged the nest of pillows all around him. They told us they were there for just that reason, and to call them again if we needed.

A few hours later, Ken was dead. Mum sat with him and told him she wasn't far behind. She brought Nicole in to see Ken, which Nicole didn't want. But mum insisted. Nicole had been his live-in caregiver for five years. She was burnt out and wanted to move on.

I stayed with my mum to do the estate work and care for her. I hired some sweet people to help with showers and cooking. I helped her dress, as she was now blind. I did the tender stuff, placing lotion on her ninety-three-year-old fragile skin.

"I thought you didn't do personal care," my mum said.

"Well I am—"

"Trying to keep me alive?"

"Yes!" and we laughed as I massaged her dry skin with gorgeous-smelling Antonia's Flowers lotion.

Over the years, whenever mum or I found a fabulous perfume, the other loved it too. It started with "Joy by Jean Patou." When mum had been out at a party, she would come to kiss her five children goodnight. I would hear the rustle of taffeta and smell her Joy. Later it was Chanel No. 5, then Bal à Versailles, which a British ballerina introduced to me. Then, Antonia's Flowers, which I found on a trip to Montauk when I lived in New York City.

I brought my mum to Westbrook Island for a month of warmth. I cooked beautiful small meals for her. Then we flew back up-north where I helped her move out of the home she had shared with Ken and into assisted living. Her choice. I had hoped she would move south with me. But mum had many friends up north and our family was there too.

After three times in the hospital in the next three months, and now needing oxygen and then morphine, mum was back in the hospital a fourth time with heart failure and pneumonia. This time she was not expected to live very much longer. I flew through a hurricane and then drove when there were no more planes flying.

By the time I arrived, the hospital staff had knocked mum out with the drug Versed because she was so upset. I asked them to wake her up so I could talk with her.

She told me she would like to try to live, if possible. My niece, a pediatrician, looked at her chart and saw that they had not treated the pneumonia very aggressively, which might have saved mum.

So, we started her on strong medicine to see if mum could beat the pneumonia. After a few days, mum, frustrated, said to the doctor, "Am I going to live or am I going to die? Tell me!"

"Well, we don't know," the doctor said. "You are a little bit of the in-between."

I slept there. I watched over her. Mum was popular, and many loved ones joined the vigil. Our loved ones took care of me too.

Mum and I would chat into the night, and one night she told me, "Don't let them wash my body."

"Okay," I said.

A few days after that, during the night, mum suffered a big unbearable pain in her back. We rang the button and the nurses came running with more pain meds. The next morning, the doctor let us know it was not going to work out for "Live." We stopped the heavy antibiotics. A few hours later we stopped the oxygen. We held mum's hand. She woke up once, giggled, and said, "Hi." Then, with a big smile, she drifted back to sleep, and hours later she drifted away.

I created a photo montage of mum and Ken to *Claire de Lune* by Debussy. I stayed ten days and arranged the memorial celebration. The church was packed. I started the process as co-executor with the fine lawyer who had helped us with Ken's estate. When I got home, alone, I cried buckets.

I miss my mum. I am in that club now, the orphan-daughters-of-mummies-that-died club.

## Christmas 2015

I made a gift calendar for many loved ones with pictures of mum and her recipes. I did not have regrets, but I wanted reassurance from mum herself, that her time of dying was the right time... so I visited a New England psychic. Through Carrie, mum told me a story about meeting up with my grandmother in spirit. My father's mother had never warmed to my mother, so when mum saw her coming near, she felt nervous. My grandmother took her hands and asked mum to please forgive her for being so cold to her in life. Mum was laughing with relief and I knew for sure I was talking with her, and that this must be what heaven is like.

Then my mum gave me many messages, praised me too; she told me I deserved to be happy. She was very loving about it.

## January 2016

My best friend, Stephan, suddenly suffered terrible panic-like cabin fever inside his huge country house which was one big artist's loft. I put him in my car and took him home with me for a few weeks. Something was really wrong with him.

# CHAPTER NINE

# Stephan in A Butterfly Care Home

My best friend, Stephan, a fine-arts painter who made award-winning experimental films, my boyfriend for a few years, and now my brother in spirit, was in trouble. I found the best neurologist in Canada who diagnosed Stephan with Lewy body dementia. I found a lonely spot in the forest and I screamed.

Was it Parkinson's disease with dementia? Or was it Lewy body dementia, which meant that Stephan presented with dementia first, and Parkinson's presented a little later? We weren't sure. Due to the debilitating Parkinson's side of his disease, I knew Stephan would not be able to escape a care home, not for long. How could I give him what he wanted most? Freedom! I was his POA and he was my POA since forever. We trusted each other and we still trust each other to this day.

Stephan's mountain town of Summerville in southern Quebec had its own cheese store and bread bakery and "cheap night" at the tourist auberge when all the locals, many artists and writers and filmmakers came from hiding out in their hills to dine and drink and table hop. Stephan and I had both built charming houses there. I sold mine as it was an investment I found while collaborating on a film there. He built his after he visited from Toronto one year. Now, twenty years later, he was not safe in his fabulous 50-foot x 50-foot atelier with his many large format paintings and windows that reach high and wide for views of the hills and the sky. I tried to manage things for him in his atelier. Home health was disturbing his stubbornly solitary life style and he was very frightened in the night. He could no longer paint. He needed Parkinson's medications four times a day and he could not cope with taking any medication at all. Parkinson's levo-carb was a miracle drug. I saw It stabilize him. It replenished the dopamine he was missing and I could see the ups and downs of mood, panic and cognition as the drug entered and left Stephan's system four times a day.

I had lived far to the south for many years and now I took two weeks at a time to set up a way Stephan could live in his house. I subjected his big house to a new expensive exterior renovation to prepare it for sale. At least people were around. Finally, his friends told me it could no longer work especially as winter was coming. Maintaining his beloved isolation could mean he might go outside and the door might close behind him and he probably forgot his key and I had visions of him frozen in the snow because no one would see down his hilly driveway. He could not drive any longer, which he could not fathom. Decline was happening fast. The best assisted living Home in Summerville was recommended. They could give medicine and tend to his weight loss. He agreed to it because he believed it was a holiday house, like in Europe where room and board were part of his childhood vacations.

He stabilized and recovered and he gained weight. He walked to his ice cream store after lunch each day, often with someone I had hired to check on him, or a friend, but sometimes alone. Staff became worried that he would elope or get lost, but he did not, and his many friends of twenty years reassured the facility directors that everyone knew Stephan and he would not get lost because everyone could see his decline in stature and memory. The town was watching out for him. Never the less, the administrator insisted on placing an alarm bracelet on Stephan. No. I said no. They decided he was too declined in memory for them, and they threatened to send him down the road to a locked facility. No. No. No. I said. But they were too worried about publicity, their reputation, should he wander away. I reluctantly agree to try the bracelet. A dear friend of Stephan's placed the bracelet on his wrist and in the morning a nurses-aid found the bracelet cut off in his garbage can. They were furious. He apologized to his friend saying it was too tight. He was sorry to have offended her about her gift. He was after all the perfect European gentleman. But the staff accused him of destroying the bracelet on purpose, defiantly and maliciously. I thought they were the ones that were behaving maliciously. They insisted he go to the locked ward immediately. They gave him three days. I flew up and I escaped him. His art student from Toronto came too and we cared for him together until he and I got on an airplane.

We made it across Canada to British Columbia near his daughters. Stephan and I stayed in a motel for ten days and tried to see if we could find a retirement community close by his daughters, who welcomed him, but not to live with them. We found an expensive independent living community. It was fabulous, however, and that lasted a whole year. During that year I visited many times. The daughters and their families were hesitant to have responsibility for Stephan. One daughter was a social worker at a geriatric hospital and I thought that was a plus. I was wrong. She advised her more loving sister to try to get out of any responsibility for Stephan. When no daughter would sign a banking POA, I continued to administer every detail of his accounts while finishing the renovations on his house in Quebec. I tried to explore the future. He would need a humanistic dementia home in BC for when we could no longer navigate his daily life for freedom. There was one I approved of in BC with a long waiting list. For now, he had great meals and medication management and home health checks in his independent living community with enough services to support his freedom and wellbeing. I enrolled him on the wait list for the best movement disorder neurologist and that waitlist was nine months long. Canada had long wait lists, except for cancer and heart disease. Dementia and hip replacements could wait. I say ouch to that. Stephan's grandchildren loved him and this was reassuring to me. Stephan kept telling me that his daughters had their own lives and they could not help him. He was right but I was still thinking they would visit him anyway. They stopped visiting him.

## Humanistic dementia units in the world:

**Hogeway** in the Netherlands, a whole, 5-acre town that operated in special normalizing ways.

**Beatitudes** in Phoenix, Arizona USA, radically personalized loving care. These two places cost $10,000 a month, beyond Stephan's budget of $4500 a month.

**Baan Kamlangchay or "Home for Care from the Heart" in Chang Mai Thailand:** This was affordable, each person had a full-time companion and this reminded me of elephants having the same lifelong companion in Chang Mai. Beautiful! Although Chang Mai was wonderful, it was too far away. I would be abandoning Stephan if I took him there. My life was in the USA.

**Dementia Care Matters in the UK**, developing special personalized emotional care. Dr David Sheard returned my call. He was profoundly interested in Stephan's difficulties. He was starting to form Butterfly Care Homes in Alberta, Canada, the province beside British Columbia! Another waiting list, of course, but dementia care was subsidized at only $2,672.00 a month in Canada.

The Butterfly Household Model for those living with dementia—trained care workers in radically feelings-based dementia care. Dr. David Sheard taught us that someone with dementia had acute emotional intelligence. In training, we learned to walk in their shoes, right beside them, as their companions from here on out. They respond to emotional care by people, who feel and act like their best friends. Life could be meaningful, validating, and full of love. Some professionals want to dismiss this concept because it sounds too much like playing at hippy love. Not so. Being with those living with dementia in an authentic way is much harder to achieve than playing at love, because it has to be tough love with ourselves. We have to face things we don't want to face in order to become authentic enough to earn their trust. That kind of love is real and multicolored, like all fallible vulnerable human love.

I knew this was right when I saw the words "feelings matter most in dementia." This could not be more true of Stephan. He was now raw and vulnerable. He was a "feeling" being.

I knew it! I knew it with Uncle Leo's stroke and dementia. Now I was studying how to do it better for Stephan. His need brought me this great gift of how to achieve his impossible wishes as his best power of attorney, his trusted one. I had found a group of people who felt like "home" to me. I came to dementia class very lonely. Not just because I was unstoppable in trying to find the right care path for my friend, but because I had been ostracized in Westbrook Island.

I rushed to this class in Alberta Canada to help Stephan. I didn't realize, at first, how right it would be for me. To be person-centered meant to work out a better consideration toward myself too, because, without that love-yourself-better piece in my puzzle, I wasn't quite as real as I wanted to be: real enough to stand before a person living with dementia and attract that vulnerable and sensitive one to my natural gift of holding hands, and giving a really good listen to their heart. This class was healing, the best fit for my spirit at this moment in my life.

In these studies, I was reminded of acting class, of my neuro-linguistic programming therapy (poor name for great therapy), "Actualizations" training with Stewart Emery, and Baba Muktananda's weekend meditation retreat. At a weekend retreat with Elisabeth Kübler-Ross and the Bear Tribe in the San Diego mountains, we searched for ways to stop suicides among Native American youth. There, a medicine man told us the number of neurons in our brains were identical to the number of stars in the universe, letting us know how connected we really are to everything and to the universe within each other. I was reminded of my hospice training. Reiki training.

Why was I thrilled to be in this class? It was most certainly a refresher for all those experiences. Everyone there shared the goal of becoming more authentic, of understanding how to simply "be." And how that can open you up to "being with" someone with dementia, attracting love and connection. This class was a match with my first mantra for my film career: to create warmth and erase coldness. I was able to created intimacy, and it resonated with the audience. People felt things in a darkened theater. There was a privacy to it. I could connect with people in that way then too.

Dr. David Sheard taught us that people living with dementia were acutely emotionally intelligent. They were "feeling" beings. The poetry of Maya Angelou spoke to David. He resonated with her idea that people with dementia will forget what you said and forget what you did but they will never forget how you made them feel. Dr. Maya Angelou showed us that a person with dementia would connect with us when we could feel with them, face them transparently with all our human flaws. The work David asked us to do was to remove our defenses and our walls. David's training demanded this of us.

I gained a clearer road to a better way of giving from my four weeks (over the course of a year) spent in Edmonton Canada, across only one mountain range from Stephan! I stayed at the convent where Dementia Care Matters trainers taught us. I stayed in a nun cell! Walking the corridors where nuns once roamed in pursuit of holy perfection reminded me of my own religion: the pursuit of excellence in my early schooling. The four visits over the course of a year felt like heaven.

Teachers, David, Peter, and Sally, conducted a series of classes that re-trained nurses how to feel with their patients. I sat, the odd one, "the American," in a room full of nurses who were struggling with how to face and remove learned detachment. How could they overcome drill after drill on hygiene and other regulations as the first line of action, turn the paradigm 180 degrees to people facing people, eye to eye. Fear-based sterility, the fear of real punishment that could come from placing those important hygiene rules second in priority, was hard to brave. Yet it was asked for, and the sooner the better.

Hygiene could be used to hide behind tasks and control residents' comings-and-goings in a facility. Vulnerable people sensed control acutely. This kind of arm's-length care was lonely and isolating to residents of any care facility. Controlling, task-oriented behavior toward residents in today's institutional settings, was evaluated by Dementia Care Matters in degrees of mild to acute forms of abuse. This accepted form of abuse was hard to see for some people … until they saw it. Tying Maddy to a wheelchair was very extreme, solving nothing for her. Do you see it? Connecting with her might have solved everything. Is it easier said than done? Very easy for some, but not so easy in a system of care that's based in fear.

Guardianship rules are similarly medical and

law-based—fear-based. That's when everyone is covering their butts.

Mid-training, I visited a Butterfly Care Home in Edmonton. I spent an afternoon connecting, holding hands with one particular resident, eating a piece of cake together, and chatting with staff. I was welcomed there. The team leader told me that the colorful stuff of everyday life all around—the staff's everyday clothes, for example, with things pinned to their clothes—enticed a vulnerable one to play with them; the homelike atmosphere was packed with many shared activities, toys and dolls and the peeling of vegetable and the folding of laundry.

"You would think some germs would get passed around," he said. "Yet, this is the first year ever that this household didn't have the usual outbreak of flu or pneumonia." He was surprised. Endorphins? Immune systems strengthen in these colorful, touchy-feely places of belonging where staff are our best friends.

It takes at least a year to retrain nurses, certified nurse aides, activities managers, cleaners, and all staff to be the most open and loving people they can be. It is hard to undo a uniform-wearing, task-oriented, hygiene-centered focus in staff. Some are naturals and long to undo these habits, undress themselves to become authentic. Some would best leave a Butterfly Care Home, where they can no longer create a club based on a control hierarchy. Yes, it can be political too. It's easier said than done, creating a Butterfly Care Home that points to a very high degree of wellbeing in its vulnerable, raw, and lost residents.

This is how persons living with dementia, and all elders, can thrive. This is a dream come true for me: a team that strives for the same thing, that strives to become aware of and then quell their urges to control everything. Nurses connect with each other and their residents based on a shared belief in creating authentic warmth and erasing coldness. Once they feel this, they can never go back to their old ways. This has been my natural way in advocacy, and I am deeply validated here.

To be with a person living with dementia is to walk in their shoes. In staff orientation for Butterfly Care Homes, Dr. David Sheard's congregate living standard, there are exercises that unveil a person. I recognized these exercises from acting class, exercises in which an actor can become aware of herself, real enough, emotionally naked enough to be authentic. This means being brave enough to face a fellow actor and face an audience. Authenticity is what attracts us all to one another. There are tools, words, scripts, intentions, and subtext in acting, and all these are nothing but bad acting, without self-awareness, authenticity, and the courage to remain open.

The brave ones at Dementia Care Matters take the first steps in training staff in how to change their paradigm. In weekly staff support sessions, one member of a Butterfly Care Home at a time, from maintenance person to head nurse, must share the emotional landmarks that have defined their lives. Not only does it open us up to our fellows and make us a team, we now understand inside ourselves that these kinds of strong landmark memories are the last memories to leave a person living with dementia. This "I allow you to know me" brings the team into friendship. They want to support one another, the same way they support their residents.

We, as staff, will have also created a "living will of landmark memories" for a time when we, ourselves, might have dementia, so some future caregiver can know us more deeply; know which memories create happiness and which memories plague us.

Staff at most facilities today are not aware of how controlling they are. They are taught to stay separated. Uniforms alone reek of authority. Once they recognize this, they cannot go back to controlling elders. They know for sure that it causes unfathomable loneliness in a person living with dementia. Finally, with this training, staff can no longer withstand being controlled in their personal relationships, either.

Going from a license to control others and hiding behind tasks to being truly yourself in front of elders, giving up controlling them, is so much more of a commitment and so much more meaningful than a staff member would know before going into this training. It's personal.

"You really did it to me, David," a nurse said to Dr. Sheard. "I got divorced because of this training! And I don't want to go back to the way it was here, or in my marriage." So, she was pissed off and grateful at the same time. Yup. Authentic.

David Sheard performed the exercise for us. He told us the emotionally defining moments of his life and gave us a great example of showing the courage to let it all hang out about who he is.

When someone lets you know them that deeply, you cannot help yourself. You love them. People with dementia have no veil. They are raw. They are extra-perceptive. They see you! When you see each other that vulnerable, you cannot help it. You love each other.

After two years of advocating for Stephan to stay free of institutions, I was able to enroll him in the first Butterfly Care Home in Toronto, Ontario. It was time, because, after two "freedom" years, his care had become a twenty-four/seven matter. This last year we formed our tiny team of loved ones, including his beloved students in Toronto, augmented by care workers, but we could no longer cope.

Stephan did not like it at first. He definitely wanted to run away. I stayed beside him. I am grateful that, slowly, Stephan could feel the welcome, become a resident where feelings matter most, where there were no locks on doors or restraining medicines, where Stephan was heard and touched, and loved. He engages with others now. He is at home.

I feel happy, because my instincts about managing the care of all vulnerable people, especially elders, has been validated by my studies with David, Peter, and Sally, and a room full of nurses, some of whom made the leap to authentic personal human connection, some who couldn't.

I would like to see guardianship become far more person-centered in these ways: Less "guarding" and controlling, and more validating, encouraging, and collaborating.

Guardianship is a last-resort solution for very difficult

situations. Sometimes it is necessary to place someone in a controlled environment like a nursing home or a locked ward. Could those places can achieve a paradigm shift too?

Dementia Care Matters trainers are disrupters in the world. They evaluate and train all care institutions into much more validating and humanistic environments.

This is what I suggest for both wards and guardians: that, we in government, in the courts, in hospitals, care homes and related adult protective services agencies engineer this paradigm shift; that guardianship be treated and administered as a calling of support, collaboration, and yes, authentic friendship. Balancing reform is needed.

Can "who to trust" start at the top levels of power and influence? I hope for this, as I continue to collaborate with, validate, and care for those who ask me into their lives.

# CHAPTER TEN

# May I Suggest Some Changes?

How can we make changes to the American system of guardianship? The law reads well, with a strong moral code that respects everyone in this process, but it often does not translate into trustworthy practice for vulnerable people, especially elders, or respectful stability for guardians.

## Humanism: keeping up with the times: More about Stephan

Dale Bredesen's book, *The End of Alzheimer's*, shows that not all dementia is progressive dementia, and some can be reversed. Stephan definitely has dementia. Maddy's so-called dementia (terror) was reversible in my experience of her.

Not every person living with dementia needs a guardian. I believe in voluntary guardianship where the elder does not lose their civil rights. This is as perfect for a person living with dementia as for a sharp-as-a-tack elder.

I never needed to declare Stephan incapacitated, yet he cannot remember that he takes medicine once a day. He takes it five times a day! He has trusted me with his money and his wellbeing for years and in our shared past, he helped me out of some hard moments in life too. So, our understanding and trust remain. It was developed through time. Trust is "feelings-based"—memory isn't required.

Even though Stephan was in this Butterfly Care Home against his wishes at first, I held his hand and watched over him while he acclimatized to the idea that he now needed twenty-four-hour care. He told me he understood that his home care team could no longer cope. You can bet your bottom dollar that nobody on the staff controls Stephan in any way. Controlling care is out of the question for him. When staff strapped Stephan into a chair to safely give him a shower, he lashed out. He couldn't bear restraints. Who can?

Stephan is raw, emotionally intelligent, and extra-sensitive, and he, himself, teaches staff the approach he wants when they don't seem loving enough toward him. He helps them too. He folds laundry and sets the table and prepares the breakfast with his kitchen buddy. He is loved in this Butterfly Care Home. He doesn't need restraints or drugs, and the door is not locked. Stephan no longer feels the need to run away. He tells me he's okay where he is.

I have learned much by studying Naomi Feil's validation breakthrough technique. This therapy proves that the most seemingly "difficult" vulnerable person is reachable, and Naomi's book, *The Validation Breakthrough*, shows many examples of how to heal so-called behavioral problems and communication chasms.

## Why I want voluntary guardianship (as many Europeans do)

Voluntary guardianship holds the guardian responsible, but the elder does not lose any civil rights. Losing your civil rights feels like punishment.

In Germany, people don't lose their civil rights, and guardianship is temporary. Unlike in the United States, guardianship is easy to reverse in Germany.

A voluntary guardianship holds the court-supervised power of attorney/guardian or the professional guardian accountable. It strives to keep the vulnerable person protected and respected.

## Feisty elders

If an elder is fighting her friends or family, because she does not want to go into assisted living, please consider this: Is it truly time? Look for other solutions. Find out what's behind the resistance. Solve problems. Don't force things. In time, I've noticed, the elder will want to move. They'll see that life could be better in assisted living. That said, make sure the assisted living company is truly person-centered. There is much false advertising. (See Butterfly Care Home Quality of Care guides in the "Terms and Resources" section.)

There are trial weeks. A person can try out assisted living for a week or two. Place some personal belongings in the guest suite. Have a relative or person they trust spend time with them there.

Promise that they can return home—and mean it—before the experimental visit takes place.

If there are dangers with money, a guardian is charged with protecting the money and shielding the person from alleged theft. It's easy to freeze money, to place money with the trust department of a bank so the money is restricted until things can get figured out. It is not always conscious exploitation.

You can be sure that the vulnerable ones are hiding money and valuables in deep, and not-so-deep, places inside their home.

It's easy to gain the trust of an elder. Include them! Hear them. Take this person with you when you go to the bank about these transactions. Involve them in the safe guards. Find agreement.

## Respecting an elder headed for a crisis:

The other day, a very creative judge met with guardians and told us a story. He saw that an elder fell in love with a man in another country, whom she had not met in person; she was sending him money so he could travel to live with her, and they could get married.

In forming an emergency temporary guardianship to stop these actions, the judge removed her civil rights, which included the right to marry.

She was in love! She wanted to marry. She was very angry with the judge.

So, the judge told her, "Okay, I'll restore your right to marry and I'll marry you myself." She was delighted. Then he added, "You tell the man to come down here. Tell him, the judge will marry you." The elder never heard from the man again. She was sad and protected.

Sometimes love is not true love after all.

Sometimes an elder will turn on their well-meaning caregiver, their trusted one, for no reason at all. Ah, but you see, there *is* a reason, and you as fiduciary must find it. There is something you are not hearing. You must learn more. The time given to them, the attention, the all-important validation that this elder matters to you, can unlock those mysteries. Naomi Feil could achieve trust, and she wrote of her experiences with elders to show us solutions in her book, *The Validation Breakthrough*. Dr. David Sheard tells us elders have "feelings", not "behaviors." Behaviors are feelings that have not been resolved. Feelings are valid. Explore the feelings, and a solution can be found.

If someone is violent to themselves or others, a plenary guardianship would be necessary. Isabella threatened to run down the elders around her with her wheelchair. Her deeper truth could not be changed. Isabella was bent on getting her life back so she could overdose. It is simply against the law to knowingly give her the right to commit suicide.

Leo wanted to take his rifle and walk in his beloved field one last time and then shoot himself. We couldn't let him do that, could we? We are the ones that locked him up that day. The problem was that he was violent with Thelma *before* he had a chance to do it, and he was forced into a system of locked wards. No one could get him out of that system in the early 2000s. Yet somewhere in our minds, we think, "Too bad he didn't go out and shoot himself."

Today, we have more loving caregivers and more loving environments for elders coming to a town near you.

## The feeling of home

If we know, if we suspect, we must try to prevent suicide. We can hold someone's hand. We can validate them. A place where their feelings matter is called the "feeling of home." We must try. Bring someone back to free will, the innate home within. This is the most important job of any fiduciary, which actually means "trusted one."

There is always a reason an elder, especially an elder with dementia, wants to go home. It's not the physical place. It's something the elder is feeling. They want to feel at home. The feeling of "I want my mum and dad." The feeling of sharing warm food. Cuddling in a bed. Yes, some dementia care homes permit staff to cuddle with residents in bed. It's harmless. Some will find cuddling radical.

You discover what "home" means to someone. It takes time. It takes observation, clues, investigation with colleagues and family. It takes connection. And home means belonging, connection. "I need my mum. How will I get through this day? I can't, without belonging with mum." If there is no mum, the caregiver can say "belong with me, then." This person needs to be emotionally safe. Dr. David Sheard and Naomi Feil both teach this. If guardianship is a collaboration, as mandated by law, guardians must have these skills. Validation training must be part of guardianship training.

A woman who was not feeling well, would not come to the lunch table at a small dementia care home that my wise friend Karen came to own. Karen allowed me to practice David's charting for evaluation of ill-being and wellbeing inside her care home. The resident came into the room, a living room/dining room and sat in a corner on a soft chair. After a while, I sat on the footstool and asked if I could bring her a little bit of lunch. She nodded. So, an aide brought some scalloped potatoes in a bowl and I placed it on the footstool, as if it were a table. I let her be. I went across the room. She had a bite or two, and then ignored her lunch. I came back and sat beside her in the big soft chair. She whispered her secret, "My asshole hurts." I went and told the nurse. They had not realized this elder had a physical problem, and one which was now easy to remedy.

This is something that we all want. Validation is respectful connection. It is "you matter." It is the unraveling of defenses, anger, hurt, listening through those layers until a vulnerable person will tell you what's really going on.

Everyone wants validation. A sense of belonging. To be heard. That's the real meaning of home, and when it's missing, the words "I want to go home" are heard in many households of the elderly across the world. They may even be in their own home. It's the feeling that matters. We live in wellbeing when we matter to one another.

It's shocking that, when we're at our most vulnerable, we could be treated like a suspect, evaluated by strangers, sent to court to stand before a judge, and placed in a nursing home against our will because someone else pinched money from us, neglected or emotionally abused us, isolated or ghosted us into submission, and then took more money from us.

I don't think someone who has been through neglect, abuse, or exploitation to the degree that quality of life is destroyed needs to be prisoned for their own protection. We can shield and protect in far kinder ways.

## Guardianship in the world

Different systems of guardianship pay guardians differently; there are different laws and value systems. Some governments take monies from the estate of a living ward. Some do not. Guardians are paid for welfare cases from government coffers. Below are some examples.

The following information on guardianship in the world and the different systems quoted from the International Guardian Network, international-guardianship.com. Guardianship systems are detailed by country on the Guardianship Systems webpage, international-guardianship.com/guardianship.htm.

## Sweden

"There are two kinds of such measures available in Sweden: 'god man' (*good* or *fair man*; mentor) and 'förvaltare' (administrator). Plenary guardianship was abolished in Sweden in 1989.

"Mentorship is the key measure in case the person concerned is in need of formalized decision-making assistance and the mentor is primarily (ideally) considered as an assistant—the [vulnerable] person concerned must consent to the legal acts the mentor performs unless such consent is impossible to obtain due to the person's health condition or in case the act concerns day-to-day household transactions. The measure has no influence on the person's legal capacity per se. He/she retains the right to enter into legal acts. In relation to certain legal acts, the mentor must obtain permission from the Chief Guardian (e.g., buying/selling real property, buying shares). The person's right to vote and marry is also unaffected by the appointment of a mentor.

"The major difference between a mentorship and an administrator-ship is that the person in the latter case is deprived of the right to represent his/herself insofar the matter at hand is within the administrator's assignment. The appointment of an administrator is a last resort measure—an administrator shall not be appointed if the person's needs can be met with a less intrusive measure, including the appointment of a mentorship. The measure must also be tailored in accordance with the person's needs. The person's consent is not required in order to appoint an administrator and the administrator does not need the person's consent to perform legal acts on her/his behalf; however, the administrator needs to obtain the Chief Guardian's permission in relation to certain acts, same as in the case of a mentorship. The administrator has exclusive power to represent the person in all matters that are covered by the appointment and the person concerned cannot, without permission from the administrator, enter into legally binding acts albeit she/he as a principle rule maintains the right to dispose of salary in case, she/he is employed. An administrator-ship does not affect the person's right to vote or to marry."

## Canada

"The general trend in Canada is away from the use of court-appointed guardians/guardianship in favor of finding and using more flexible, sensitive, effective, and humane alternatives that respect both the adult's wishes and the adult's network (family, friends, etc.). Supported decision-making alternatives are growing by leaps and bounds, especially for people with developmental disabilities.

"Guardianship is not quite a dirty word in Canada, but it is definitely seen as undesirable, but a necessary evil.

"Safeguards are provided by adult protection legislation and the system of oversight, offered by well-funded and established public guardian and trustee services. Canada has a well-established, publicly funded, and effective universal health care and social service apparatus, which provides an array of services supporting progressive policies and legislation. The provisions of the UN Convention, especially Article 12, are already being endorsed in most jurisdictions, but particularly west of the Great Lakes where things like supported decision making have been recognized in legislation and policy for nearly twenty years."

## The Netherlands

"Every guardian is entitled to a fee, to get his expenses reimbursed and a reward. A number of partners and family members do not ask for this. The fee is regulated by a decree from the Department of Safety and Justice (former Department of Justice). In case the adult has insufficient means to pay the fee (a regular fee is €1,100 per year), special social security from the city will pay the amount. Jurisprudence has made it clear that once the guardian judge has ordered a measure and granted a certain fee to the guardian, the local authorities are not allowed to question the necessity of the measure or the size of the fee. The point of departure is that the tasks can be done within seventeen hours per year. And all other normal activities of the guardian are covered. For extra activities, the rate is €65 per hour, but the judge has to agree beforehand.

## England

England gives €350 per ward, per year. Poor isn't it? A guardian (called a deputy) is surrounded by special visitors and general visitors hired by the Office of Guardianship, who are medical and social workers paid on a contract basis.

## Germany

I like their plan. They pay the humanistic fee of €1,848 a year per ward, paid by the Department of Justice: $2,139 per ward and the guardian must be attentive. Here is the entire German system:

# Resource for Second World Congress on Adult Guardianship

| |
|---|
|  **Country:** Germany |
| **Population: 81.8 million** |
| **Number of people under Adult Guardian/ Guardianship: approximately 1.3 million** |
| **Relevant legislation** <br><br> German Guardianship Law is a federal law and part of the German Civil Code. |
| **Key terminology** <br><br> "Rechtliche Betreuung": supported decision making <br><br> Ward: person under guardianship |
| **What types of guardianship exist? (personal welfare/ financial affairs)** <br><br> No full (or plenary) guardianship. There is a strong focus on supported decision making. Limited guardianship for court specified duties is possible. In the majority of cases, guardians are responsible for oversight of medical treatment and financial management. Wards retain full legal capacity. |
| **Aside from personal appointments, who has the power to appoint an adult guardian?** <br><br> Only the Probate Court (Betreuungsgericht) has the power to appoint an adult guardian. |

**What criteria does the court need to consider when deciding the need for a guardian?**

Where there is a concrete need, the court can appoint a guardian for a person over eighteen years old, who, as a result of mental illness or disability, is incapable of managing their own affairs. A guardian should not be appointed against the "free will" of the person concerned—but the court has to consider whether, as a consequence of their mental illness or disability, the ward is capable of "free will."

**What is the potential duration of an order?**

At most, seven years. In an emergency, a temporary order can be made for up to six months.

**Can a person under guardianship seek review of a guardian's appointment and/or a guardian's decisions?**

The decisions of the court of 1st instance (Betreuungsgericht—Amtsgericht) to appoint a guardian can be reviewed by the court of 2nd instance (Landgericht). The ward can represent themselves at such hearings. A guardian's decisions are not generally reviewed by the court. However, if a conflict of interest develops between the guardian and the ward, or the guardian fails to respect the rights of the ward or otherwise acts inappropriately, the court may act to replace the guardian.

**Who can be appointed as guardian? (e.g., family members, private guardian, private body, public body)**

**Family members, volunteer guardians, professional guardians (for example, lawyers), "Betreuungsvereine" (non-profit advocacy organizations) and public guardians.**

**What are the responsibilities of an adult guardian? (e.g., what principles or guidelines must they comply with)**

All decisions made by guardians must take account of the ward's past and present feelings and wishes, benefit the ward and be the least restrictive option available. By law, every guardian is obliged to be in personal contact with his/her client and to cooperate with them.

Guardians are guided by the three principles of Necessity (no guardian's decisions in areas that the ward can manage independently or with the support of family/friends); Autonomy (the ward should lead a self-determined life to make as many of his/her own decisions as possible); and Preservation of rights (every adult has fundamental rights, including to marry and to vote).

**How are adult guardians monitored and/or supported? (e.g., overseeing body, support for volunteer guardians)**

Guardians are required to submit annual reports to the court. These annual reports are reviewed by guardianship auditors employed by the court. The guardian also needs court approval for 'special decisions,' including major medical treatment decisions. In general, it is the duty of the guardianship court and the Office of the Public Guardian to support the guardians. Further, non-profit advocacy organizations provide support for family member and volunteer guardians.

| **Does an existing enduring power of attorney (personal welfare/financial) remove the need for guardianship when capacity is lost?**<br><br>Yes. An enduring power of attorney is possible in the areas of health care and personal welfare, as well in financial matters. |
| --- |
| **What costs are associated with guardianship and who pays? (e.g., application costs, court costs, yearly service fees)**<br><br>It is free to make a guardianship application. And, in most cases, adults under guardianship do not pay court costs. However, if a ward has monetary assets of €50,000 or more, they are required to pay an annual court fee of around €500. The Ministry of Justice pays an annual guardianship service fee (€1,848) to the guardian on behalf of wards with limited means. Otherwise, the ward pays the fee. |
| **Additional comments (interesting elements … not covered above)**<br><br>Germany's current adult guardianship laws were developed with full awareness of the crimes and discriminations committed against people with disabilities during the Nazi period of 1933–45. The probate judge plays a central role under current law. They hold responsibility for fundamental |

decisions in relation to the ward and they have personal contact with the ward. Further, guardianship hearings are accessible to all, taking place in private houses, hospitals, and old people's homes, as well as in courts.

## More stability for guardians

In this American system, guardians simply do not have the kind of time needed to do their best work. Yet, they're the trusted ones. So, this is why I say, take time off the table by removing the requirement to run an entrepreneurship. Create a salary system for guardians that would improve quality of life for vulnerable people by improving time challenges for guardians.

Guardianship is a calling, not a pyramid scheme. Some guardians have a BMW; most guardians are unable to make ends meet. This should not be an entrepreneurial system, but salaried, collaborative, and yes, healing. More stability for guardians creates more stability for their wards.

At present, the guardian fees are taken from the ward's monies—if the ward has money. By petitioning the court through a lawyer for the hourly fees, a guardian receives permission from the judge to take fees from the ward's bank account. Those fees can be $20 to $85 an hour. I make a budget first, before deciphering if the guardianship can afford to pay me, but it's not wrong for a guardian to charge $85 an hour. The guardians I know are very poorly paid because so many cases are pro bono.

Sometimes a guardian will strategize to balance the pro bono cases by billing the wealthy wards excessively to cover some of the guardian's losses, without the ward's knowledge or permission. Violet sensed it, resented it, and freaked out when she wasn't respected or heard about her money or believed about her friends and family having integrity. Collaboration about how your money is to be spent is part of the code of ethics.

Those who were trying to petition the court to get Violet out of the guardianship were then accused of being exploiters. Did the court not care to hear from them? Where was the evidence? Suspicion and fear. Negative, reputation-destroying strategies. Character assassination in whispers, but little or no due process. Violet did not want to be protected from her nephew and his lawyers. She was begging for them to be heard and to help her out of the guardianship which was intolerable to her and maybe unnecessary.

This way of getting paid, it feels like Robin Hood. Take from the rich and give to the poor. What's wrong with this picture?

I believe this is done in concert, in whispers, with judges, who rightly feel sorry for guardians because the balance of pro bono cases is unfair. I understand why it's condoned by judges and their clerks, auditors, and guardianship lawyers. It really does risk real conflict of interest, when those in this system agree with occasional overpaying of fees to clearly underpaid guardians in this uncomfortable, hidden way.

Most often, this is done without agreement from the ward.

Was the judge deceived by the guardians? The guardians created a naughty crazy Violet for him. They created various exploitation scenarios. Any discussion and collaboration with the court system in the matter of guardianship fees and operating budgets can become sealed and confidential. It sure makes me squirm. The ward senses, by instinct, that they are powerless and probably being used against their will. With real communication, and supported decision making between a ward and a guardian, both can find stability and then trust, but not in the present system.

America is a free enterprise country, you say. I don't think free enterprise works ethically when it involves the most vulnerable among us. Decisions about their money are one of ways wards are not considered. This leads to open permission for guardians to overuse their authority, even though mandated communication, listening to a ward's wishes, and collaboration is the way to grow trust. Developing trust, real trust, is supposed to be guardianship's first goal. It is the law.

It also leaves open something else that often happens. Guardians are unfairly accused of exploitation and conflict of interest, without cause, by a ward or their family. My suggestion is: do not use the ward's money to pay guardian fees. Then any accusation of exploitation by a guardian will not be easy to believe. The system is in denial about how guardians are paid. It's disrespectful of guardians.

There must be ways to remove the possibility of real and imagined conflict of interest from the guardianship system. Most guardians resist any conflict of interest around money.

The system must offer guardians adequate security and a fair wage.

There is some desperation involved when guardians take extra money from the wealthy ward to buy clothes, food, and dental services for the less fortunate. This also keeps a worthy but impoverished guardianship enterprise open for business. The system imposes extra stress upon the guardian. This system hurts guardians and rich wards.

We must collaborate with our wards and do as they wish as long as their action doesn't harm them or others. Keep them safe in the *least restrictive environment*. The system must better support these ethics. Otherwise 'safe' becomes a rationalization for isolate and trap.

I have shown "safe" taken all the way to "overly safe," as in an unnecessary nursing home with restraining medications. That is not the least restrictive environment. Recovery is the rule, but it's not enforced. In truth, it's rare to recover someone who's very self-destructive. Elders can be self-destructive but that is rare too.

My experience tells me it's possible, even easy, to recover an elder who, like Maddy, hoped to thrive once more. If it's too dangerous to recover the money, leave the money behind, and take the person away from the exploiting situation; quality of life is more important than money. Negotiate for the recovery of quality of life in elders and in those living with a dementia.

I hope these stories have shown that vulnerable people still can make good decisions. They have the right to make decisions, even bad ones, the results of which can be minimized when supported with the skilled guidance of the guardian. In Canada, "supported decision making" in collaboration with a vulnerable adult is the law.

If recovery is not expected here in the United States, a guardian can be tempted to use excessive authority. I see many elders recovering their self-determination; and even with dementia, there are many decisions emotionally intelligent elders can weigh in on. It is their human right. Because this can be time-consuming for a guardian in a system that demands running competitive, entrepreneurial business models with too many clients, the ward is often cheated out of time and being part of the decision-making process.

The questions regarding conflict of interest, real and imagined, should be taken off the table by arm's-length salaries for guardians—salaries that are not dependent on the assets of a ward because guardians then become territorial and compete against one another for rich clients. I was warned that the guardians would throw a snake on my back if I interfered, and they did. It may have looked to their jaded minds like I was trying to steal their ward. I was not. I was checking on the wellbeing of their ward, and unfortunately, I saw a guardianship strategy I wish I did not see. I could not un-see it, so they had to shut me up. The golfer buddies had to shut Maddy and me up. Bullies all with influence, using adult protective services, and lawyers to do their bidding.

The guardians for Violet (in concert with the court) were driven to financially harvest this widow to pay for seventy-five pro bono cases. They strategized like Robin Hood. They found a solution to stay afloat in a sick system that doesn't support them, and so, they took advantage of their wealthy vulnerable ones. I don't think they felt good about it.

I do thank them for helping me realize that the system had placed them in this corner, and there they found strategies to work within the system. Ethically remiss, yes. Are they to blame? The system is exploiting both guardians and rich widows and widowers.

## Melanie

I recently met with one of the many good guardians in America. In some states, the law has limited the number of wards cared for by one guardian to thirty, at any given time. Melanie has her hands full with sixteen wards. She is dedicated, so they receive more attention than is required by law, but not as much attention as she or I would want.

Two wards can afford to pay her. Fourteen wards are pro bono. After nine years, she does not make a living wage. She's supported financially by her husband, who remains encouraging. She has an LLC status to protect their assets, should she get sued.

Melanie, like most guardians, does an excellent job. She cares about her wards. She's organized, resourceful and professional. She's kind and respectful to everyone surrounding each guardianship. She's not allowed to discuss her cases with anyone but the judge through reports submitted by the lawyer for the guardianship. She submits to scrutiny of all her reports, by the auditors and the clerk of the court. She is meticulous to the penny. If Melanie were actually paid for her work, it might look like this:

### Sixteen wards
Three wards passed away.
Three new wards:

Month 1 & 2 x 3 wards x $1,000 (fee for work on initial reports to court, plan for person and property)

$3,000

Month 3 onward—3 wards x $200/month x 10 months

$6,000

Thirteen wards stable x $200 a month x 12 months

$31,200

### Total year's salary for sixteen wards

### $40,200

This proposed salary structure aims at equalizing the field. In this scenario, Melanie is paid for both impoverished wards and wealthy wards. Standardized fees would be the order of the day. The guardians who think they can get rich will go away.

It will remove competition for elderly clients who are wealthy and create more equality with pro bono cases. Guardians will be paid a decent wage for each ward, whether a person is rich or poor—there's no difference.

Once salaried, every guardian can opt for less wards and be relieved to find more time in their day for listening and creating more wellbeing for their wards, which will reduce the 'Sophie's Choice' wrenching feeling of too many wards and not enough time and bring the satisfaction they truly want in their work. It's a public service, and it deserves respect from us all, including a decent wage.

A ceiling of $60,000, with no more than twenty-five wards a year, would say to any person entering the profession: "We do this as a calling." A guardian can never hope to get rich, but one can at least have a degree of security while doing this job with a million responsibilities and the credo "First do no harm" as in all medically adjacent work.

## How can these guardian salaries be funded?

### Option 1

You could have Medicare, Medicaid, and social security pay the guardian salary system. This funding would be based on the number of guardianships per state. "Public" guardians are funded and salaried by the state; all professional guardians should be similarly salaried.

## Option 2

Guardian salaries could be covered by a specific estate tax, which is granted only after the death of a ward and matched by state budgets. These funds could be run like school budgets. Where do teachers' salaries come from? How are the clerks of the courts paid? Or salaries for guardians can be part of the circuit court's budget, as in Europe.

While a ward with money is living, their money cannot be harvested to pay guardianship fees and other expenses. After they die, I've been told by my elders, it won't matter to them. There could be a tax on the estate that goes into the special funding of guardianships and guardians. This needs to be matched by state funds. This could also be funded and administered in a city by a city budget.

The estate tax could be based on the number of years under guardianship. This might be calculated based on the cost of creating and maintaining the guardianship, or not. It could be less complicated, such as a small, flat percentage of an estate. Donations by very wealthy families could also be welcomed, as is done in hospice organizations.

These are a few reasons why I feel that guardianship can be paid for by a special estate tax probated after death, and not on the date of declaration of incapacity. Keep the money working for the ward while they're still alive in the name of mercy, quality of life, and respect for an individual. It's easier to listen to someone's wishes, if their wishes do not jeopardize your fees.

**Option 3**

North and South Carolina, Florida and Texas, New Mexico and Nevada have far more guardianships than The Northern USA. Many Michigan and New York elders travel to live in the southern states, where its warm even though they have no family close by. Guardians watch over many of these elders at the request of family who live far away. Create county or city budgets on a per ward basis. Some counties have many more wards than others.

## Don't do this

While the United States is a free enterprise, capitalist country, please do not use vulnerable people to fund a business venture. Don't do this to our elders. It's easy to see how this can look like taking advantage of them. Even if that is actually a rarity, it feels uncomfortable. In the name of freedom and the pursuit of happiness for all, our vulnerable people deserve ironclad trustworthy support.

## For pro bono wards

There needs to be a welfare fund for pro bono guardianship expenses for personal needs, eye care, dental visits (like the toothache resolution or relining of Sophie's dentures), or a hearing aid, which is not covered by Medicare or Medicaid. There is a whole world of need among indigent wards. Guardians need financial help here.

## A successful guardianship business

The guardian who received the guardianship of Sophie onto her roster, has a different structure in running her business. I already knew Marilyn K. was a master of creative solutions. She figured out how an eighty-year-old indigent woman could leave a hospital without having to accept a guardian. For two months the woman was refusing to leave hospital and refusing a guardian. The hospital needed a guardian to make the decision for placement and to sign papers requiring the patient to leave. I did not like the hospital's reasoning and it was my very first offer of a case, so I had less resources and solutions. I stepped aside. I heard that Marilyn K. came in and suggested that the hospital simply transfer the patient to *their* nursing home where the patient could live at a less expensive rate. Problem solved. Everyone was happy and there was no guardianship. I loved hearing how that case worked out!

Marilyn K. has run her business as a Board-Certified Geriatric Care Manager for sixteen years. She was a registered nurse before that. I saw immediately that this person had a depth of soul. I could feel her ethical nature and her true yet very quiet wish to connect. She listened. This year I asked her how she ran her business. She has straight forward services, with fees published, as a Geriatric Care Manager with nine employees. Guardianship, she understood wisely, was a last resort solution. When necessary, she was also a registered professional guardian and could bring a client into guardianship. Sophie was a bro bono case. Marilyn was not going to be paid for this ward. Even if I did not tell her more than "It's me. I am the problem. Not Sophie. I can't go on and I need a good guardian for Sophie;

I believed she listened between the lines and, with her keen instincts, decided to help me. It helped me greatly to know Sophie had the best guardian.

Now, years later, I explained to Marilyn, my theories about guardian fees needing to be arm's length to avoid real and imagined conflict of interest. "How do you make money as a guardian?" I asked.

She said her Geriatric Care Management Business was the umbrella that supported guardianships. The need for guardianship is rare in her world as she finds creative solutions, if she possibly can, to avoid guardianship. Sophie and a few others are managed under the umbrella of her Geriatric Care Management business which is contract based and voluntary on all sides. Marilyn let me know she had to come to terms with actually taking money for doing something she loved so much.

A friend told her this, "If you are proud of what you do, then you have a right to charge."

She has responsibility for nine employees who love what they do. "Money comes in and money goes out. We make ends meet and that is enough for me." she tells me.

This is an ethical way to have a guardianship business inside a broken system.

# Life and death decisions

Almost always overworked in this entrepreneurial system, guardians need change, not just so they can earn a fair wage, but so they aren't burnt out or too stressed when a life-and-death situation comes to the fore. Guardians don't want to be too tired when pursuing knowledge about a person in order to make life-altering decisions.

Sometimes there is no family member, even distant, when someone is close to death but with a slim chance of recovery. A guardian is called in and asked by the court to find information, anything and anyone who could shed light on this person in limbo. The person may be in a coma or delirium and cannot speak for themselves. This is a huge ethical job for a guardian.

The first part is gathering information. What would this person want if they could speak? So, you find neighbors, clergy, doctors of the past, and undertake detective work. The next part is making a decision based on the knowledge gathered, and if the decision isn't clear, asking the court to examine the case and help make the decision. The ethics committee at the hospital and any person with knowledge are asked to present. A guardian is never alone in this matter. A guardian will not make any hasty decisions. Sometimes the doctor treating the patient will not bother with this legality and quietly decides to let a person go.

Agnes, in the assisted living facility, caught a urinary tract infection, again. As Agnes's guardian, I knew she was in a delirium because a UTI got out of hand and she was in sepsis.

The assisted living facility called an ambulance and they called me.

The ER doctor, believing that delirium was her normal state, planned to forego treatment and let her go. A glass ceiling in not treating elders can be a confidential budgetary policy of the hospital. Elders are expensive.

I told the doctor that this was not her normal state, that she must have an infection. I asked the doctor to try to save Agnes.

He ordered comprehensive tests and based on the results; intravenous treatment was started. Agnes's grandchild volunteered to be with her in the hospital for three days. Because she received some very strong and specific antibiotics, Agnes recovered and in spite of being eighty-nine years old, Agnes lived another two meaningful years with her loving family.

Yes, we could have let her go, but Agnes wanted to stay. She wasn't ready, and her family wasn't ready. The doctor needed the knowledge I gave him.

In assisted living, one must be able to ask for help. Agnes was shy about asking for help in the bathroom and that is how she got the UTI. The nursing home side of this continuing care community would take care of her in a delicate, respectful manner, whether she asked for help or not. It was time for Agnes to move; we talked about why, and she agreed to it.

By spending three days in the hospital, Agnes qualified for Medicare for recovery time in a nursing home. And during those ninety days, we were able to apply for Medicaid long-term care at the same nursing home. This worked out, and Agnes was not charged more than the amount of her social security check in the future.

Maddy's case was different. Because Maddy was admitted to the hospital for "observation" by her power of attorney (rather than for "extreme pain and treatment," which is what her nurses thought), Medicare was not obligated to pay for rehabilitation in a nursing home. So, Maddy was charged $35,000. If Maddy's admission had been more appropriately changed to "treatment for pain," this money would have been saved. This could have been corrected. But no one was listening, no one was hearing that Maddy was in pain or honoring her right to self-determination.

Their insistence to declare Maddy "incapacitated" blinded them to Maddy's true experience. Instead of helping an elderly woman in pain, they declared war on her and her helpers. Maddy therefore was placed in "protective custody". She requested home health aides because she was afraid. Her POA's complained about the cost of nighttime companions. Yet, $35,000 of her money was needlessly spent. The need for control and authority over Maddy was becoming a lethal concoction.

When Maddy was admitted to the hospital, it was a moment in time that included a decision about life or death. The wrong decision was made. I knew it. I could do nothing about it. I was stopped. I am sorry, Maddy.

Something about the health care system and elders definitely stinks. Elders seem disposable—let's take their money or save "our" money from being drained by them. I can't stand that. Can you? It's not just a matter of ethics. An elder can always say whether they wish to live or die. Just ask. Hospice is so humanistic, loving in this matter that elders relax and often graduate out of hospice to live well again.

Check your hospital's elder policies. Know that they may lie about it. Guardians know truths like this only by experience. Hospitals do not want us to know their glass ceiling for elder disposal policies.

I believe in elders. They know what they want or, at least, what they don't want. Always check on a loved one in a hospital or assisted living or dementia unit or nursing home. Their safety is not guaranteed. Their wishes are often swept under the rug.

## The grey time frame

*How do we support guardians in life-giving*
*exploration before guardianship?*

If it were not so incredibly difficult to get out of guardianship in America, I would not be teaching people, especially elders, about ways to avoid it.

There is a grey area, and you can see it in Maddy's experience. She could have recovered from her crisis. She had the will to thrive, and she knew what she wanted. She needed a little bit of supported decision making and to recover from self-imposed malnutrition, because she felt her money was gone (it *was* controlled by others). I believe Maddy's so-called "paranoia" and extreme fear were based in truth and not in her imagination. She knew she was being disposed of; hence, her cries for help. She needed therapy to decipher why she talked gibberish to Betty and Jerry, sabotaging herself. Maddy seemed sensible and level-headed to my team. Her gibberish sabotaged her case for self-determination, ensuring the inevitable stressors that we all knew would lead to a hastened death.

All guardians come across cases like this. Geriatric care managers have permission to operate for wellbeing; guardians have the will to make these kinds of improvements too. Guardians are not certified to collaborate with elders without the "court appointed" status. But guardians are asked, many times a year, to meet with a neighbor who says, "I am worried about an elder in my church" or "Pretend you are already her guardian, [the court takes at least a month to establish a guardianship] so the daughter will stop stealing money."

So, people come to us. I showed a few cases where guardianship was avoided. In the case of my friend, Dora, I went to the Department of Children and Families and applied for Medicaid on her behalf without the court behind me. To do this, I needed confidential information. I knew that I was trustworthy. Most guardians are trustworthy. The public needs reassurance, however. Let's give it. Let's make it as transparent as possible.

Because our guardianship system's norms have been so imprisoning, fear-based, and hard to reverse, my goal was always to see how the person could recover before the three evaluators came in to decide the level of capacity and the court case could proceed.

**The grey time**—I want this to mean "Let's try to improve this person's wellbeing before we call them 'incapacitated,' before adjudicators, doctors, psychiatrists, and social workers come in and report and, sometimes too quickly, declare a person incapacitated."

Guardians see the inside of a person's home, and this must be felt. Adjudicators meet this person, stranger to stranger, for an hour—it makes for a limited evaluation.

Therefore, I am looking for a reporting system for the grey time frame. The "not yet time." The "maybe we can avoid guardianship" time.

**Transparency**—what's needed is "someone" to tell, and a little legal safety for the guardian during this time. May I suggest a witnessing protocol?

As a guardian, I have come across an elder in crisis, but I don't think it's necessary to create a guardianship. Can we look and see? Can we have a court contact person?

For example, the court monitor of guardians, who is usually a social worker, could witness, offer acknowledgment, and give permission to bring a situation out of crisis before evaluations. A frozen bank account, perhaps? The court is in the know. But not anything as extreme as an emergency temporary guardianship with all the drama that goes with it.

It could be a non-ETG, with much more privacy for the elder; something that doesn't stress an elder by the sheriff showing up and serving them with papers. That is scary! There could be a facilitated transparency from the guardian to the court without chastisement for the unauthorized exploration.

Perhaps the court has some ideas about this. If guardianship were not so difficult to reverse, in the USA, then this grey time frame might not be so legally dangerous for guardians, who have no permission from the court to help the people they meet. It happens all the time. Let's support it.

I believe people living with dementia should not be declared incapacitated at the drop of a hat. Doctors and guardians are too busy to really consider how cruel a hasty diagnosis really is. Dale Bredesen's book, *The End of Alzheimer's*, shows us a great deal about misdiagnosis and reversible dementia. *The Spectrum of Hope* (an optimistic and new approach to Alzheimer's Disease and other dementias) By Gayatri Devi, MD, offers much more specific and humanistic ways to treat those living with dementia.

This grey time frame is when someone might be recovered without guardianship. Could this be legislated to save the expense and end-of-the-line loss of civil rights, which is demoralizing, stressful, and against quality of life?

We must have a way to protect guardians and vulnerable people in crisis for a period of three months when improvement from the crisis can be made, with a chance of avoiding guardianship.

The Pioneer Network (https://www.pioneernetwork. net/) is working for a paradigm shift to truly person-centered approaches, toward the goal that all elders matter, which includes person-centered guardianship and supported decision making for all vulnerable people. This is a growing movement— it can't come fast enough for me! Dementia Care Matters has a big role in making the same change today. It's the gold standard in emotional care, emotional safety, and the return of wellbeing in a vulnerable person. This kind of respect and caring must be applied to guardianship as well.

I have never asked for a fee for a requested exploration and often I have quickly and simply resolved the problems and pointed someone away from court-appointed guardianship. My need to advocate is free of charge because, for now, ethically, there is no fee structure for guardians resolving cases before they come to guardianship. We're not supposed to do it. We *all* do it, however.

For example, a young gentleman, recovering from kidnapping and abuse, had extra monies owing retroactively from social security. He needed assisted living. So, to protect his money, Charlotte, his social worker, asked me to consider guardianship for him. She was the healing force, supporting his return to wellbeing. I made a few phone calls. I found a trust company that managed annuities like social security income, which must benefit only the recipient and no one else. Some paperwork was needed to resolve this for the young man's safety. The trust company became the "representative payee" for his social security check, which, in his case, paid fully for his monthly room-and-board and personal needs. This solution took an afternoon and some faxes. No guardianship was needed. This work is often a no-brainer for a guardian, who works closely with the laws regarding social security.

This grey area (where guardians work as guardian angels to resolve matters for safety and wellbeing) is sometimes easy, but always, guardians are vulnerable to being accused of things that can harm a valued-and-needed good reputation. If a family member decides to intervene, if there is money in contention or a greedy person stands to lose something by the vulnerable one's money becoming protected, then the guardian can be attacked, and their reputation challenged. This can get messy. This can be deeply hurtful to a guardian.

Sometimes, when greed and animosity enter into the matter, interfering with relatively easy improvements and protections for a vulnerable person, a guardianship should be seriously considered. If there could be a court guardian monitor to witness the exploration a guardian is asked to perform during this grey time, then the decision to go for guardianship—to protect the vulnerable one from someone who protests—is transparent. Protecting the person-centered guardian must be a priority too. Within a new system of stabilized salaries for guardians, with a ward's monies used only to increase wellbeing in the ward, guardianship could become a much more user-friendly public service.

## Ethics committee/support group

No one stood by me when I was accused of exploitation by Maddy's handlers. I propose an ethics committee/support group made up of guardians to sort out the confusing way things sometimes happen. We need both the ethics review, clarification, solutions and reassurance or private chastisement— in other words, real support.

I needed support. I deserved support. Too much fear in my fellow guardians did not allow for that. I was to be silenced. I am not silent, however, am I? Let's tell everyone!

Some of my colleagues could have stood up for me in a united front once they learned of the confusing circumstance and of my dilemmas. Guardians could advocate for guardians. This is needed.

Did I do something wrong? I did not call Adult Protective Services to declare suspected emotional abuse and neglect by the Picards. I wish I did, but I did not. I did not trust Adult Protective Services. They favored and helped the guardians who wanted to push me out of their territory. Therefore, I hoped the parties could work it out confidentially, in Maddy's favor and according to her wishes.

Why didn't I call? I didn't want Maddy to end up under the control of the territorial, competitive guardians, David, or Marianne and June. I didn't want them near any vulnerable person I knew.

If there had been a more supportive environment, an ethics committee/support group, a protected place … I might have been able to voice my worries about the territorial guardians. I might have healed this situation if I could tell someone who understood the confusion. When I was forced to step away, my fellow guardians/friends might have stepped forward and helped Maddy. I begged my colleagues to intervene. But there was too much fear that what happened to me would happen to them. Transparency in a sick system is needed.

## Exploitation by the system and by individuals in society

Francis, my lawyer up north, suggested that I ponder and write about various ways to quell exploitation. "This would be of great value to the people reading this book."

So here goes:

## Family exploitation

In the area of exploitation under $5,000, for example, where a family member takes too much money because they may feel they're not being paid enough for the care they're giving or have become impoverished by caring for an elder, there could be some kind of special therapy and resolution. I can see a face-saving, humanistic problem-solving strategy for this kind of exploitation.

I think we can solve those cases. We can stop this kind of exploitation by validating the caregiving. Help those caregivers out of their hole. The collateral damage of a person falling into crisis extends beyond the vulnerable or elderly person toward burdening a family caregiver. Because of minor exploitation by the caregiver, the case can descend toward unnecessary guardianship. Everyone needs help, especially the caregiver.

If a son or daughter cares for a parent and they're poor, needy, burning out, and tempted to exploit the parent, rather than jail them at $40,000 a year, let's give them a bit of money with some gratitude thrown in; it will create validation and healing and support them to continue providing quality home care.

A social worker can be hired and added to a voluntary guardian to help the family member dig out of their emotional and financial caregiving crisis. In this day and age, when a catastrophic illness can place someone and their family in the poor house, the solution above may seem too idealistic. But landing ill people and their caregivers in the poor house in this society is common and as cruel as it gets.

## Emotional abuse

The elder has signed over their fortune to someone and then regretted it. This now-enriched friend or relative strongly discourages friendship with others, which is called "isolating." Anyone who comes into the circle is pushed away by the people in charge. They control the elder by demeaning, humiliating, and punishing them, by ghosting or neglect, in order to keep their windfall safe by weakening the elder. As energy is diminished, feelings of hopelessness and depression creep in.

This is emotional abuse, often related to exploitation. Therapy could work here to a degree. So, could placing the money in an arm's-length trust account until all is clear, with the money secured to benefit the elder while alive.

This probably requires a court process, but if the windfall recipients agree to these safeguards and a voluntary guardian is assigned to the elder, all can be resolved.

If the money grabbers are hostile to these ideas, they are not listening to the wishes of the elder or respecting anyone; they are greedy without remorse. Go ahead and protect the elder to the full extent of the law with an arm's-length trust account for the elder and deeper protection with more supervision of the court. Please listen to the elder and help them escape this cruel punishing fate.

## Negligent guardian

If the guardian is neglecting an elder or stressed for time, and therefore not listening, then the process above can apply to a guardian. In England, court monitors are called "visitors" and trained as a check-and-balance to the guardianship. They also support guardians in their difficult cases while scrutinizing them at the same time. It is difficult for a guardian to exploit because they are seriously scrutinized.

## Exploitation by guardians

Everyone in the system knows guardians are not paid in a fair way. There is denial about the vast number of required pro bono cases, and guardians cannot receive a fee for those.

Wealthy clients are rare. It is often uncomfortable to ask the court to take money from a ward to pay a deserving guardian, knowing that gaining a wealthy client is rare and therefore that elder is at risk of being over charged or grossly overcharged which must be called exploitation.

Most guardians struggle to make ends meet. This is a plea for a paradigm shift in a system that disregards guardians. I argue here for creating a trustworthy guardianship system. Even with a fair wage and stability for all guardians by an arm's-length salary system, there are ways of stealing money and assets from wards, even though guardians are heavily audited by the clerk of the court. A new system of guardianship monitors would help as witnesses in the field. These monitors, (called "special visitors" in England) can see the assets for themselves. It's hard to hide assets, such as cars, houses, and art. It's easier to take the cash or jewelry that all guardians find in all kinds of hiding places. Of course, this is against the calling of trusted ones. Most guardians take pride in their honesty. Most are honorable. A very few are in jail.

If something is disputed by the family, assets must be audited again. Assets are always audited by the clerk's office, and the court needs to give permission to sell assets, such as art, stocks, and houses, and to buy things such as funerals. A salary system at arm's length and guardian monitors would help solve any real or imagined exploitation by guardians.

I repeat, because of the competitive entrepreneurial system of guardianship businesses, elders with money are at risk of being held inside that system. Hence, we need salaries for guardians, to ensure there is no need for funding by rich elders. The focus would be on life enhancement, which is what most of us guardians, who lift many from crisis, want.

## Real exploiters: criminals

Stop those who are simply greedy and without ethics, who are taking assets from a vulnerable adult, intentionally, without any remorse. Call the police. Freeze the assets, bank accounts, and real estate, and put those people in jail. Sometimes the construction trades exploit in this way. Sometimes a neighbor. Sometimes a stranger who knows how to make an elder fall in love with them. It's hard to discover these cases until the shame-faced elder is in crisis. The elder is madly in love with the person or euphoric or distressed, becoming ill and headed for a crisis to the ER and more trauma.

Too often, a temporary protective action turns unnecessarily permanent. When the danger is resolved, once the protection of assets and improvement to wellbeing is in place, the plenary guardianship should be stepped down to the least restrictive options.

Voluntary guardianship is an agreement to recover. Heal the elder with true regard for their wishes and then seeing how to recover the monies and assets that may have disappeared months before. If the money cannot be recovered, then gain charity services if needed. Guardians know how to access social services. And still, plenary guardianship can be avoided because the guardian has permission on all sides to access the legal system that will deal with the offender. The offender will know that the guardian is watching over the victim of exploitation. Offenders can be dangerous.

## Extreme exploitation and abuse

There are dire cases where guardians and extreme shielding are strongly needed. Elders and other vulnerable souls can be exploited, sexually abused, and physically abused. This speaks to the enormous fortitude and wisdom of many guardians who encounter these cases and protect their vulnerable ones very well. Guardians and the courtroom and many healers are needed here.

## More on geriatric care managers and professional guardians

A ward has been declared an incapacitated person and loses some or all of their civil rights so that the guardian can gain the authority to make decisions. I do not agree with elders losing their civil rights just because they are old or in danger of exploitation. However, a suicidal woman with MS is a danger to herself, and her rage makes her a danger to others. Even she can gain back a few of her rights, but most guardians will say, in this case, they need the authority to save this person from themselves. I am sure we all agree with this very sad situation as a guardianship. The job is about making decisions. If the decisions are harmful to self or others, a guardian will take charge and make better decisions. Hopefully healing decisions.

Theoretically, the guardian must involve the ward, or the

ward's loved ones, as much as possible in decisions … if they have time. Unfortunately, guardians in this system must take on too many cases in order to make ends meet. It's a paradox: they don't have time, so their authority is used as convenience about "no time to collaborate." This must be corrected.

In many cases, I see guardians take charge. I do not see much collaboration, due to the number of cases and the stress of time. So even mandated collaboration that's insisted upon in the statutes is rare in practice. This can change.

**A geriatric care manager** has a contract with a plan and a fee structure that is pre-signed by parties involved.

**A guardian** relies on petitioning the court through a lawyer in order to get paid.

Both guardians and care managers see inside a home. Both resolve things like squalor, self-neglect, and malnutrition by hiring others. Neither does personal care, so home health agencies and assisted living facilities are constantly selling their services at networking meetings with guardians and care managers.

If there is little or no money, guardians will be forced to take on transportation to appointments, personal care, shopping, and matters of personal safety. Some guardians refuse to transport wards; I transport wards.

Guardians take in all vulnerable souls who are dangerous to themselves or others and must make very hard decisions about locked facilities and other protections.

As I have said, I feel strongly that, with detective work and deep listening, a guardian or care manager can find a solution without imprisonment. It takes time to find solutions in collaboration with an elder. Very often people are imprisoned for the convenience of others, who don't want to spend time on finding other solutions.

Guardians would like to spend much more time with each elder and feel guilty having to choose who gets attention on a particular day and who doesn't.

Care managers can charge agreed-upon fees and spend the time discovering solutions in collaboration with and on behalf of the elder. There may be a crisis looming, but there are rarely "Sophie's Choice" challenges—one getting attention while another does not—as in a guardian's more chaotic life.

A care manager will present a case to lawyers to start guardianship proceeding if the case is a dangerous one. A guardian will be chosen by lawyers and the care manager. Three doctors or other professionals must declare the person incapacitated. This takes at least three weeks.

A guardian is often chosen to manage the situation in the interim with no protection for themselves by court or any mandate. A guardian is told "Take another guardian or person of trust with you. Do not enter this situation without covering yourself. Have a witness." That said, a guardian can be seriously punished by their own colleagues, lawyers, and the court if something goes wrong at this time. Therefore, fear presides.

A care manager will not risk a dangerous situation. Probably a guardian should not risk it either. Some guardians are able to let a person remain in danger in order to protect themselves; I am unable to do this. All guardians are in danger with one case or another some of the time. All guardians agree to be in danger, and they develop a thick skin.

## Broken system:

Adult protective services, is an agency that I fear. Perhaps they found me naive, and yet, most of the experiences I've had with adult protective services have been unhelpful. They are quick to blame, to judge, to condemn. Adult protective services is a fear-based culture. They do see many horrendous situations. Guardians do too. When I speak about this, I want to ask the reader the advocates to forgive them, acknowledge that this is hard core stuff.

Guardians do not realize they are not embraced or helped by investigators at adult protective services. In a meeting with investigators and social workers, I stood up for guardians as honorable. There was a big groan. Guardians seem to be dismissed as a necessary evil. I am determined to shine a light on guardians. They are a needed public service. They are most often, angels in this system.

There is little room for improvement in the life of a ward because of the conservative, prudent, extra-cautious way a guardian must relate to them. There is a great chance of recovering and re-achieving quality of life in the hands of a geriatric care manager.

A guardian must be conservative and prudent (read "restricted") in making choices for a ward.

The wishes of wards are mandated to be heard, but those wishes are not often considered in practice because the ward's rights are gone. In the USA, others have the authority to make decisions for them. Because both guardians and wards exist in a system of fear and restrictions, recovery is the goal in theory, but it is not practiced. Recovery of rights is the ideal, yet we do not try very hard to achieve it.

Guardians resist change, including innovative or experimental therapies, sometimes as ordinary as vitamins. The doctor orders everything. Legally protecting those involved is the rule of the day. "Cover your own ass" is a wise rule in this particular legal system.

I want to innovate. I hope to make guardianship user friendly, more trustworthy in the public eye (because most guardians deserve the badge "trustworthy"), more affordable, and far more useful to the aging population.

Elders who find themselves in this system currently may suffer greatly. I repeat: Very few belong in guardianship.

# TERMS AND RESOURCES

## Terms

**AIP:** Allegedly incapacitated person. It now means adjudicated incapacitated person.

**Baker Act:** Initiating involuntary and emergency commitment for psychiatric examination under the *Baker Act.*

**Blanket bond:** Insurance coverage that protects against any losses due to guardian dishonesty.

**CPAP:** Continuous positive airway pressure. The main treatment for obstructive sleep apnea.

**DNR:** Do not resuscitate. A legal order not to resuscitate in the event the heart or breathing stops.

**ETG:** Emergency temporary guardianship. A guardianship declared quickly for three months if a vulnerable adult is in imminent danger. Authority is given to protect the person and the financial assets.

**Indigent:** Suffering from extreme poverty.

**MRI:** Magnetic resonant imaging. Medical imaging technique to generate images of the organs in the body.

**Plenary guardianship:** A full guardianship with civil rights removed and full authority given to oversee and manage the person and the property.

**Pro bono:** Work undertaken without charge.

**Restoring:** The act of "restoring" a person's civil rights. Can go beyond that to restoring the ability of someone to manage once more, their own affairs. Most elders deserve to retain their rights, with a little help and supported decision making.

**Voluntary guardianship:** A power of attorney monitored by the court. I like voluntary guardianship. The client and guardian can see if they are a good fit. The court oversees the guardian and the ward doesn't lose their rights. The vulnerable adult must be able to agree to this and sign for themselves.

## Resources available

A circle of support should be expanded to all the people a vulnerable person wishes to see. Isolation and paperwork regarding seeking permission to visit are common. Family and friends must be welcomed, (even those who have been causing damage, maybe while under supervision). There must be healing opportunities in those families and social work support.

Not everyone needs guardianship; they may need just a little help. Good guardians will listen and guide and support their wards to make decisions for themselves.

Canadian Association for Community Living.
An advocating force toward protecting choice

for those with intellectual disabilities and safeguarding inclusion. cacl.ca

- Dr. David Sheard and Dementia Care matters. The Butterfly Household Model. dementiacarematters.com

- Positive Approach to Care. Dementia care expert and advocate Teepa Snow. teepasnow.com

- Helen Sanderson Associates. International training, development, and consultancy team working to embed person-centered practices in the heart of communities and organizations. helensandersonassociates.co.uk/us

- Jenny Hatch Justice Project. Supported decision making as an alternative to guardianship.jennyhatchjustice project.org; jennyhatchjusticeproject.org/training

- **Center for Guardianship Certification.** Excellence in guardianship standards. https://guardianshipcert.org

- http://www.inclusion.com/fliers/PATH%20MAPS% 20Toronto%20March%202019.pdf Two tools taught by the inclusion Network that can assist in identifying an individual's goals and life desires are MAP and PATH. These tools can be easily adapted to adults and are one hundred percent person-centered.

  International Guardianship Network. A non-profit and non-governmental organization providing support, information, and networking opportunities for guardians. international-guardianship.com

- Marsha Forest Center. Development of future leadership for inclusion. marshaforest.com

- National Resource Center for Supported Decision-making. Information about the right to make choices. supporteddecisionmaking.org

- Rachel Aviv, "How the elderly lose their rights," *The New Yorker*, October 9, 2017. An article about Nevada guardianships and about people losing their civil rights simply because they are old. newyorker.com/magazine/2017/10/09/how-the-elderly-lose-their-rights

- The Pioneer Network. Advocating new culture change in aging. pioneernetwork.net

- 16Personalities. Learn to understand others by learning about personality types. 16personalities.com

- What it means to "hold space" for people, plus eight tips on how to do it well. by Heather Plett https://heatherplett.com/2015/03/hold-space/

- The Geriatric Care Managers Association https://www.aginglifecare.org/

# Book list

- Dale Bredesen, MD, *The End of Alzheimer's: The First Program to Prevent and Reverse Cognitive Decline* (2017). About reversible dementia and testing more thoroughly.

- Noam Chomsky, *Requiem for the American Dream* (film, 2015; book, 2017). See the documentary film or read the book.

- Naomi Feil's books about validation therapy, including *Validation: The Feil Method* (1982) and *The Validation Breakthrough: Simple Techniques for Communicating with People with Alzheimer's and Other Dementias* (1993). We allwant to be validated and belong. Naomi Feil writes of ways she has been able to reach elders whoare upset, disturbed, or antisocial. vfvalidation.org

- Atul Gawande, *Being Mortal: Medicine and What Matters in the End* (2014). Addressing hospice care, the current state of care, age-related frailty, serious illness, and impending death.

- *On Tyranny-Twenty Lessons from The Twentieth Century* by Timothy Snyder

- Dementia Care Matters, "Evaluation of a Memory Care or Any Care Home." Relevant to true person-centered guardianship practices of the future.

- http://www.dementiacarematters.com/pdf/Making ToastHandout2016.pdf

- *Slow Medicine: The Way to Healing by* Victoria Sweet

- *The Spectrum of Hope, an optimistic and new approach to Alzheimer's Disease* by Gayatri Devi, M.D.

- *Finish Strong. By Barbara Coombs Lee.* Advice for people in the final stage of their lives.

# THANK YOU

- Thank you to Laura C., a retired judge whom I've known for 40 years. Thank you, Laura, for telling me I was most unsuited to the profession. You are right, and wrong too. I am an idealist and an artist who hopes justice can prevail, even though I have little trust in the present system. "One must learn that the law has little to do with justice." Laura didn't think I could learn that. Not sure I want to.

- Thank you to Mary, my mentor guardian, who could not teach me to advocate less. She was a good guardian, gentle with her clients and respectful with all business and court dealings. She gave me a ward and a job taking her wards to appointments, watching out for them, gaining better lives for people, and thanks for our confidential chats.

- I had three wards of the court. My collaboration with them and with doctors, social workers, facilities, pharmacies, families, and the court, and lawyers that I respected, was successful and meaningful. I thank all three wards, and to the other vulnerable persons described here, who I helped avoid guardianship or who were lost in spite of my efforts. Thank you for teaching me who I am in this calling.

- The guardians who financially harvested the rich widow were created by the system, and I hope very hard that the American system will change. I thank them, too, because they showed me how impossible it is do this independent business model called guardianship.

- Thank you to my family, who supported me financially and morally through this apprenticeship. They know me well. They accept me and my fervent nature that wants to be all-consumed by justice and mercy for my clients and this project.

- I thank Owen T. in the south and Francis M. up north for bringing sanity to me when I was in total shock. These two lawyers have deep experiential wisdom. They are at the top of my list of who-to-trust.

- There are real obstacles that prevent guardians from meaningfully enhancing the lives of people. If we can help, it is the greatest feeling. Today, I go to school and learn about true and radically person-centered care for those living with dementia. This work suits me. Thank you, Dr. David Sheard and company at Dementia Care Matters, for creating a meaningful way for people to live with dementia. For me, it applies to all elders. For Dr. David and company, it applies to everyone they come in contact with. I benefit from how person-centered they are to me. David, you are the and most important person-centered icon on the planet. Thank you for all you will do in the ripple effect to support all the vulnerable ones in the world me.

- Thank you to Karen, best assisted living administrator in the business, and Charlotte, MSW, and Abby, parish nurse, they have all been my friend. Those friendships supported my survival at some very messy and painful moments.

- I thank Mia H., a talk therapist, for helping me find my voice again.

- In writing this memoir, I thank my fellow writers and early readers, R. Connor, M. Cain, J. Chaps, P. Matteo, H. Watts and C.J. Marsh, M. Isaac, M. Lee for reading through many drafts. Their patience and impatience were as crucial to this work as my determination to jump over my own hurt in order to complete these stories, in the hope that others can be better informed about their choices in vulnerable situations.

- Thank you to Balboa Press for the resonant support I need in exposing my story.

CPSIA information can be obtained
at www.ICGtesting.com
Printed in the USA
BVHW080459151219
566639BV00001B/13/P

9 781982 239169